ALEX McLEISH

ALEX McLEISH

The Don of an Era

with ALASTAIR MACDONALD

Foreword by
ANDY ROXBURGH

JOHN DONALD PUBLISHERS LTD
EDINBURGH

ISBN 0 85976 242 4

Phototypeset by Swains (Edinburgh) Limited
Printed in Great Britain by Bell & Bain Ltd., Glasgow

Foreword

On December 2nd 1987, Alex McLeish captained Scotland for the first time in his career. The occasion, a European Championship match v. Luxembourg, was also significant because Alex became the eleventh player in history to gain fifty caps for Scotland. Natural justice is not always prevalent in football but for Alex fate smiled and he was justifiably rewarded for a career of sterling service, and everyone in Scottish football enthusiastically endorsed his inclusion in the game's Hall of Fame.

When I became involved with him as a player, his reputation preceded him — 'a great lad', 'brilliant attitude', 'a dominant personality'. Only by working with him did I come to realise that these often hackneyed descriptions were, in Alex's case, astonishingly accurate. Prior to gaining his fiftieth cap, I asked him to captain both the 'Under 21' international team, as an over-age player, and the B-international squad. Many experienced professionals would have viewed such requests with indignation. Alex, while disappointed at his non-inclusion in the senior side at that particular time, proceeded to lead the youngsters and the inexperienced with a commitment and diligence which gained him the admiration of team-mates, staff and public alike.

Alex McLeish is the epitome of all that is good in Scottish football. He loves the game, gives his all, and plays for the cause rather than his own ego. It is said that God will judge us not by our material gains but by our battle scars. Alex McLeish has fought many battles; most of them have been successful, all of them praiseworthy. Whether he is making a saving tackle, rising majestically to head clear, or threatening the opposing goal at a set play, Alex's heart and soul are always fully in evidence.

A patriot against England at Wembley, a calming influence against Bulgaria in Sofia, a stalwart against Spain in Madrid. Wherever the match, always dependable.

Alex McLeish is a gentleman, a distinguished footballer and a man of quality. It has been a pleasure and an honour for me to know the player and the man.

ANDY ROXBURGH
1988

v

Contents

Introduction

I enjoy my football! I hate losing — I always have — but the disappointment of defeat is only temporary, and somehow it makes
subsequent success all the sweeter. I've discovered, too, that this
backward look at my career has enabled me to re-live those joyful —
and sorrowful — moments all over again.

But more than anything else, compiling this book has brought
home to me how much I owe to so many people for all the help I've
received at various stages of my career. I would like to take this
opportunity to record — belatedly in some cases — my appreciation
of their efforts.

To mention but a few, in my days with Barrhead Youth Club and
Boys' Brigade football, there were Kenny Rogers and Jim Brown,
while at school my mentors included Alan MacLeod (Big Mac) and
Gibby Baird. Then there was Andy Hanlon of Rantic and Big Fin of
Glasgow United.

Those early amateur coaches were later to be followed by their
professional counterparts in the various managers I have served
under at Pittodrie, together with their able lieutenants, such as Teddy
Scott, George Murray, Pat Stanton and Archie Knox.

To all these, and to anyone whom I have inadvertently omitted,
my sincere thanks.

In producing the book itself, I am grateful for the kind co-opera-
tion of Aberdeen Journals, the *Daily Record,* D.C. Thomson & Co.
Ltd. and Sportapics/George Ashton in making photographs available, and particularly Bob Bruce, chief photographer of *The Press
and Journal* for specialist photographic work.

The season under our new management team of Alex Smith,
Jocky Scott and Drew Jarvie has started reasonably well and it's
great to be in the Skol Cup final again for the second year running.

1
Skippering Scotland

The date: Wednesday, December 2, 1987. The place: the Esch-sur-Aizette Stadium in Luxembourg — not, you might say, the most appropriate setting for a momentous sporting occasion.

Insignificant in international football terms it might be, but that tiny Luxembourg football ground will always occupy a very special place in my memory.

There was I, Alexander McLeish (to give me my Sunday name), a few weeks short of my 29th birthday, making my 50th full international appearance, and captaining Scotland in recognition of that milestone.

Skippering an international team was not entirely a new experience, for earlier in 1987 I had fulfilled that function as an over-age player in the Scotland Under-21 team and later in the B international against France at Pittodrie. But this was something else.

Leading out the full Scotland team in a competitive international is something I may never do again, but even if I'm given a similar opportunity in the future, I'll still regard the Luxembourg game as the pinnacle of my football career, the realisation of a boyhood dream — one which, over the years, must have been indulged in by thousands of schoolboy footballers.

I was on Cloud Nine when I was told that I was to be captain, and I'll always be grateful to Andy Roxburgh for his thoughtfulness in naming me as skipper for that game.

In the event, however, the match itself had a disappointing outcome, a goalless draw against Luxembourg being a less than flattering result for Scotland.

It was, of course, a game in which we were on a hiding to nothing from the outset. Even if we had won by two or three goals, any praise would have been tempered by acknowledgement of the indifferent standard of the opposition, while a bad result — such as the draw which materialised — was going to earn us a slagging.

The choice of venue for this game certainly didn't help, and in terms of atmosphere, or rather lack of it, it was one of the strangest internationals I have ever played in. Behind one of the goals, there was a high fence separating the ground from the gardens of nearby houses, and this conjured up in my mind a hilarious image, sweeping me back to my childhood days.

If the ball cleared this fence during the game and landed in one of the gardens, I could visualise one of our number approaching the householder and asking in a broad Scottish accent: 'Hey mister, can we hiv oor ba' back, please?'

To be serious, though, we can make all the excuses we want, but, at the end of the day, it was a game we should have won.

Even the poor result couldn't ruin the occasion for me, although there was one personal disappointment when I missed a scoring chance late in the game. It was a really good chance, so good that I was thinking of a goal as the ball was coming to me.

Probably I had too much time to think what I was going to do because normally when I score a goal — not that that's very often — it's a snap chance which is over in a flash.

This time, I had stayed up after a corner had been partially cleared and when the ball was knocked back in again, I timed my run and jumped just right. Out of the corner of my eye I saw the keeper coming at me and he clattered into me, but only after I got in the header. The ball, however, went just wide of the goal.

I should have scored, and the miss kept me awake thinking about it for a couple of nights after the game. Just think! Captaining Scotland AND scoring the winning goal both in the same game! Ah well, you can't have everything in an imperfect world.

I suppose being entrusted with the captaincy of a team affects different people in different ways, but as far as I am concerned, I think it has a beneficial effect.

When I'm playing for Aberdeen, and sometimes even in practice games, and a team-mate does something wrong, I tend to be a moaner — a verbal backside-kicker, if you like. I usually curse myself later for moaning, as if I didn't make mistakes myself, but that's just the way I'm made. I like to win!

But when I'm captain, whether of Aberdeen or an international team, I find I encourage the other players rather than moan at them, and any criticism I make is more constructive.

One special bonus of the Luxembourg game was that for once I was able to tell Willie Miller what to do.

Seriously though, the presence or absence of Willie from a team I am playing in does have a bearing on myself.

Our partnership will be discussed at greater length later in the book, but, for the moment, suffice it to say that when I'm captaining Aberdeen in Willie's absence, I feel an extra responsibility.

When he isn't playing, I'm conscious that people might be ready to point the finger and say, 'They can't do it when Miller isn't there'. Consequently, I'm determined to ensure that such critics don't get the chance. Happily, I usually respond to this challenge.

My earlier description of captaining Scotland as the pinnacle of my football career might prompt some readers to ask themselves whether I was forgetting another glorious occasion — Aberdeen's European Cup-Winners' Cup final victory over Real Madrid in Gothenburg in 1983.

Perhaps I should have been more precise and written of the Luxembourg game as a 'personal pinnacle', for Gothenburg was essentially a team triumph.

As such, it has been woven into the folklore of this part of Scotland, and for the players and everyone else involved, it will be a memory which will never fade. But more of that later.

It strikes me that I've been rambling on about comparatively recent events, and as this is supposed to be the story of my life so far, I should really begin at the beginning. So let's turn the clock back twenty-nine years.

2
Boyhood Days — and Coaches

Although my first association with professional football was following in my father's footsteps as a Rangers fan, I could just as easily have started off as a Celtic supporter. At different periods of my childhood, my family lived near both these clubs' grounds.

When I was born in Glasgow's Duke Street Hospital on January 21, 1959, the family were living in the Parkhead area, but one of our later moves took us to within a stone's throw of Ibrox, at Kinning Park.

Soon after I had started at primary school, we moved from there to a new Glasgow overspill development at Barrhead, where the family home still is, although my mother Jean was left a widow when my father died six years ago, aged only 43.

As their first child, I was named after my father, with sister Angela and brother Ian coming along two and ten years later.

My father, a shipyard worker, was undoubtedly a major influence on my sporting career, and one of the important things I learned from him was being able to see more than just one team in a football match.

He was a fervent Rangers fan and I can remember when he started taking me to matches, he delighted in telling his mates that I was the 'jinx' responsible if Rangers happened to have a bad result (Rangers were going through a lean spell at that time, with Celtic having things virtually all their own way).

My dad may have been rather more biassed in his younger days, but by the time he was taking me to matches, he was much more balanced in his judgements and he was always ready to acknowledge the good points in the opposing side's performance.

Because of this, I never took the blinkered attitude that some of my pals took. Some of them would never wear anything green and silly things like that.

The religious divide, as far as I was concerned, was a nonsense, and I still think that. I had pals drawn from both Catholic and Protes-

5

tant households. It made absolutely no difference to me what their religion was.

I wasn't all that unusual in thinking this way. In fact, my first experience of competitive games outside schools football was as an 11-year-old playing for a juvenile team specially created for youngsters who shared my liberal outlook.

The team was called Rantic — a blend of Rangers and Celtic — and the idea was to create a bridge between the young followers of the two big professional clubs. At least that was the aim of its founder, Andy Hanlon, although I suppose we players were too young at that time to look on it as much more than another opportunity to play football.

Andy gathered together a good team, but, sadly for such a praiseworthy attempt to reconcile the Old Firm factions, funds dried up before the project could be properly developed and the team was discontinued.

As I said, my dad was a big influence in my life, probably the biggest, although I must admit that the interest he took in my football drove me to tears on occasions.

He came to watch me play twice on a Saturday, and if I protested when he turned up for the second game on a Saturday afternoon, he would make the excuse that it saved him going to watch Rangers and then getting drunk to drown his sorrows if they were beaten. At the same time, I suppose I would have been disappointed if he hadn't shown such a close interest in my football.

Dad could be very critical of my play and I used to fall out with him from time to time. On one occasion, I remember swearing at him and then going home in tears with him walking some distance behind me. When we got home, my mother, of course, took my side and told my dad he should give me a break.

But after thinking things over, more often than not I would realise that what he had said had been right. Without the motivation which dad supplied, I doubt whether I would have got anywhere in football.

My father's father had played for Cambuslang Rangers when they were a semi-professional club and he himself played to a fairly high standard at school and junior level.

If my father supplied the drive, it was a different kind of encouragement which came from my mother. Apart from furnishing the bus fares for my football travels, she was the one who tended the cuts and bruises when I got home.

Starting among the trophies — Barrhead Youth Club team with coaches Brown (left) and Kenny Rogers.

We used to play a lot on red ash in those days, which could be a nightmare for sliding tackles, but as a part-time auxiliary nurse she was well qualified for cleaning and dressing my wounds.

You might not believe it now, but at primary school I was quite small for my age — it wasn't until I was between 15 and 17 that I suddenly started to stretch — but my lack of height didn't worry me too much, apart from the time I read with disappointment a newspaper article in which Rangers' chief scout was quoted as saying that he was always on the lookout for big, well-built boys. I couldn't get enough football. As soon as I came home from school, it was up to the field or into the street for a game with my pals.

In the summer months there was a slight distraction when, inspired by watching Wimbledon on television, we would switch our allegiance to tennis. There was a big house nearby which had a private tennis court and we used to sneak on to it and have our own wee tournament before the lady of the house came to chase us off with the help of a big black dog.

It was only when we got older that we began to appreciate some of the other sports such as golf etc.

My dad always encouraged me to be involved in as many sports as I could. I was always fairly sports-minded in any case, and being blessed with a good eye and coordination, I was a reasonable performer. At table tennis, for example, I was runner-up in the Renfrewshire schools junior championship.

But I'm getting ahead of my story, so let's get back to my primary school days.

I made my debut for Springhill Primary School while I was in Primary 6, which was quite an achievement as most members of the team were in Primary 7 and a year older than me.

Playing as what would in those days have been called left half, I scored a goal on my debut, but one of my clearest memories of that time is that the school had a wee outside left by the name of Peter Weir.

Little did I think that I would be associated with him again much later in my football career, but even at that age, Peter's natural ability was really remarkable. He was the trickiest thing I had ever seen on a football field, able to beat an opponent with one foot and still control the ball with the other as he went past him.

Springhill's greatest rivals were another Barrhead school, Auchenback, and one of their players with whom I became very friendly was Gordon Boyd, who became Rangers' youngest-ever S-form signing at the age of 12.

Really, Gordon was at that time a man among boys, although I think in later years he didn't fully realise his potential and other boys caught up on him. But as a primary schoolboy he was strong beyond his years and could score goals from 30 or 40 yards' range.

Gordon, for all his ability, was a little bit jealous of Peter, and, being a bit of a hard man, he went out of his way a couple of times to 'have a go' at Peter when our two teams met in derby matches.

Peter was in Primary 7 when I came into the team, but we parted company when he moved on to secondary education at Barrhead High School, where we became team-mates again for a spell, although I think Peter lost interest in the game for a while in the later stages of the secondary school, while for me football continued as an all-consuming passion.

By the time I was in Primary 7, I was a striker — and a goal-scoring one! In fact, I became the top scorer in the school's history with 43 goals in eleven games.

I continued to score a few goals when I moved on to Barrhead High School, where, incidentally, Gordon Boyd, Peter Weir and myself all found ourselves in the same team, but it was then that I started to move back in the team, first to midfield, and then, later, into defence.

As I was still quite small then, most of the goals I scored were with

A challenge bowls match against former world indoor bowls singles champion Bob Sutherland, himself a former Rangers player.

my feet rather than the headers which account for most of my goals these days. But I remember Gordon Boyd's uncle, who used to watch our team regularly, saying to me on one occasion:

'For a wee man, you're pretty good with the heid.'

My father had always encouraged me to 'find my man' with passes, and by keeping it simple and never trying anything fancy, I became quite effective as a constructive player and this led, I think, to me being used in midfield (to use what was then a comparatively new-fashioned term).

At Barrhead, which was a junior secondary school, I was part of a successful team. We won our league in Renfrewshire schools football two or three years running and one year we reached the semi-final of the Scottish Schools Cup. Drawn at home to North Kelvin-side, we were leading by two great goals, both scored by Gordon Boyd, but eventually were beaten 3-2.

While football was still my main interest, I didn't neglect my lessons entirely, and after getting five O-grades at Barrhead High, I moved on to John Neilson's School in Paisley. We had a choice of two senior secondary schools in Paisley and, along with most of my mates, I chose John Neilson's in preference to Paisley Grammar School because we thought the latter was a bit 'toffee-nosed' and snobby.

I got Highers in Maths and English, and although I failed my Higher French, it must have been a close thing because I was given a compensatory O-grade in that subject.

Most of my early football guidance came from my father, but I'm also indebted to a number of teachers who helped me on my way at various stages of my schooldays.

My primary school mentors might have included Andy Roxburgh if he had been on the staff at Springhill a year or two longer before being promoted to headmaster of another Barrhead school.

Andy was at Springhill while I was in Primary 5, but his other commitments restricted his school coaching activities to Primary 7, and by the time I reached that exalted stage, he had, of course, moved on.

The teacher who made the biggest impression on me at Barrhead High School was an Alan MacLeod, who, by coincidence, belonged to Cullen and happened to be an Aberdeen fan.

Whenever the Dons beat Rangers or Celtic, as they did quite frequently at that time, he used to wind us up about that.

'Big Mac', as he was known among his pupils, was always very encouraging on the sports scene at Barrhead and on occasions he was instrumental in securing the reinstatement of boys who had been suspended from school teams for minor misdemeanours.

I still keep in touch by letter with Mr MacLeod and he is always interested in hearing about how his former pupils are getting on, particularly Peter Weir.

I believe he is now semi-retired, but is back helping with the school team, and I have no doubt he is as popular with the present-day pupils as he was with us.

'Big Mac' was someone you could respect, but you could still have a good laugh with him.

As the end of my schooldays approached, I began to be aware of a slight mental conflict over my future, with my love of football tugging against the more practical consideration of finding a good job.

3

Pittodrie-Bound

Most adults can think back on an incident which left them wondering whether the whole course of their subsequent life would have been different if this event had not occurred. Fate, Dame Fortune, or whatever else you like to call it, can intervene in the strangest way.

With me, it was a car breakdown.

Towards the end of my senior secondary education at John Neilson's School, I was also playing for Glasgow United, a juvenile club which regularly attracted scouts from a number of senior clubs.

This led to me being offered a trial for East Stirling — not the

Flashback to a brief but happy spell with Aberdeen junior club Lewis United.

12

most glamorous of clubs admittedly, but to me at that time senior football was senior football and I wasn't waiting indefinitely for Rangers or Celtic to come along for me.

A United official was to give me a lift to Firs Park, but his car broke down as we were crossing the Kingston Bridge and we were held up for a couple of hours, missing the game and, I thought, my big chance to break into senior football.

Some time later, the chap who had given me the lift swore to me that that was the first time his car had ever let him down. He also commented that the breakdown must have been dictated by Fate, because by that time I had signed for Aberdeen.

The East Stirling mishap occurred during my second spell with Glasgow United. I had played in one of their teams when I was 12, but then I joined a team which Barrhead Youth Club formed to play in the Renfrewshire League and won a few honours with them — Peter Weir was again one of my team-mates. When the Youth Club team was disbanded, I rejoined Glasgow United as a 15-year-old.

East Stirling's trial offer wasn't my first connection with senior football. A couple of years earlier, following a game between Glasgow United and Hamilton Accies' reserve team, I was invited to train at Douglas Park a couple of evenings each week.

But that came to an end, when one night Eric Smith, who was Accies' manager at the time, told me that his directors had decided that they could no longer pay my travelling expenses unless I signed for the club.

When I told my father about this, he told me that I wasn't to go to Douglas Park again. 'We can't let any club put a gun to your head at your age,' he said.

The first hint I had of my possible future came in a brief paragraph which I noticed in the Glasgow *Evening Times* to the effect that Aberdeen were 'interested in Glasgow United centre half or sweeper Alex McLeish'.

But this appeared early in the 1975-76 season, and as time passed nothing developed and I came to the conclusion that Aberdeen must have lost any interest they might have had in me.

It was another successful season for United and we appeared in several cup finals at the end of the season, one of which produced a remarkable coincidence.

This was about the time I was about to leave John Neilson's School and it was beginning to look as if my future would lie in finding an everyday job rather than in the professional football career I had set my heart on.

At this particular final, though, my father was approached by a Bill Sutherland — who, by the way, I met again recently at Jim Duffy's testimonial at Dundee. After telling my dad that he was connected with junior club Rutherglen Glencairn, Mr Sutherland asked if I would be interested in playing for them.

My dad was quite in favour of the idea, but he explained that a few days later I was due to have an interview with Rolls Royce to start an apprenticeship as a technician.

Imagine my dad's surprise when Mr Sutherland told him that it was he himself who was conducting the Rolls Royce interviews.

In the event, neither the job interview nor joining Glencairn materialised, for attending that same cup final was a high-powered Aberdeen delegation consisting of manager Ally MacLeod, chief scout Bobby Calder, his assistant Jimmy Carswell (now chief scout), and area scout John McNab. Unknown to me, Mr McNab had been checking on me all season, and now, possibly spurred on by reports that other top clubs including Celtic, Rangers and Hibs were interested in me, the Pittodrie club were ready to pounce.

Bobby Calder declared the Dons' interest to my father after the game and arranged that he and Jimmy Carswell should visit my home the following evening, when, after Bobby's customary distribution of gifts to my family, I signed for Aberdeen on a provisional form.

And so my quandary over what I was going to do after leaving school was resolved. Everything just seemed to slot into place. To use a football cliché, I was 'over the moon'.

My dad, however, still had some reservations about me becoming a full-time footballer, but Aberdeen overcame this obstacle by promising to get me a part-time job in the Granite City.

This was in accounting, so my Pittodrie career started with me splitting my time between football on the one hand and working in an accountants' office and attending classes on the other.

Before I deal with the problems this caused, I must relate a sidelight of that cup final which, looking back, was amusing, but could have been disastrous for my soccer career.

It took the form of a story which Ally MacLeod told me — with great glee — many years later.

Apparently, that game was the first time that all the Aberdeen representatives had seen me play, apart from John McNab, who had been the one watching me on earlier occasions.

It so happened that the team we were playing against that night also had a big skinny red-haired guy at centre half and Bobby, obviously having misunderstood John McNab, pointed him out to the manager as the player they were supposed to be watching.

When Ally was asked for his reactions after the game, he replied: 'Well, quite frankly I preferred the one in the other side!'

Luckily for me, they finally sorted out the confusion and decided that I was the player they wanted to sign.

Back to my early days at Pittodrie. In addition to my part-time work on a day-release scheme in the accountants' office, attending classes three nights a week — which, incidentally, brought me a sixth O-grade — and playing football on Saturdays, I was doing ground-staff chores at Pittodrie — sweeping up the dressing room, cleaning boots, etc.

All this left me without much free time, but I kept up this hectic schedule for over a year until it finally came down to making a choice between accountancy and football. There was no real choice for me. Football was always going to win, with the thought that I could always go back to accountancy at a later date.

Like any youngster arriving at Pittodrie, I was bursting to get into action with the reserve team right away, but there were some more experienced players ahead of me in the queue, and to start with I had to content myself with a half-season of junior football when I was farmed out to local club Lewis United.

Looking back, though, that was a valuable experience, not only good for my game, but also a happy introduction to Aberdeen.

I thoroughly enjoyed my time with Lewis and made many friendships, some of which have endured to this day. Jocky Bremner, for example, was the team skipper and a joiner to trade, and he still comes along to my home when I need some nails hammered in.

On these occasions, we exchange reminiscences and he usually makes a good-humoured complaint about my arrival in the junior team.

'There was I, the captain after five years in the team, and this 17-year-old from Glesca comes along and gives me stick and tells me what to do,' he grumbles.

John Mulgrew, a real enthusiast, was president of Lewis United at that time and the team was run by Stewart McAra, while another of the men behind the scenes was Jimmy Hogg, who will be remembered by older Dons fans as a full back in the Pittodrie team of the late '50s and early '60s. Often helping Jimmy to tidy up the dressing room after a Saturday afternoon game was his son Graeme, who went on to play for Manchester United.

Other Lewis people of that period who come to mind include Dennis Forman, Billy Leask, Charlie Bain, Bob Bruce, who is now the *Press and Journal* chief photographer, Bobby Shiach, Jimmy Stewart and George Copland.

Apart from being a very friendly lot off the pitch, Lewis United had a good team. Then, as now, Banks o' Dee were the side by which other teams measured themselves, and in our meetings with them that season we won three times, drew once and lost only once.

I particularly remember one Scottish Junior Cup-tie — I think it was in the second round — when we travelled to meet Thorniewood United in early December.

As the game was in Glasgow, my father went along to watch it and he laughed when he told me about one of the home team supporter's remarks: 'Look at that big lanky centre half. His legs go all the way up to his oxters'.

I was accustomed to uncomplimentary remarks such as 'carrot heid', drawing attention to my distinctive hair colouring, but this was the first time the length of my legs can have been the cause of comment.

The Thorniewood tie was one of the few football matches played in Scotland that day because of bad weather, and because of this we got a special mention on television.

The tie finished in a 1-1 draw which, in the light of Aberdeen teams' lack of success against West of Scotland opposition in the Scottish Junior Cup at that time, was regarded as an excellent result.

We had had much the better of the game and looked forward to beating Thorniewood in the replay at Heatheryfold Park on Boxing Day, but could do no better than another 1-1 draw, so the tie went to a second replay at a neutral venue, at Carnoustie Panmure's ground, where we lost 2-1 just after New Year.

That defeat signalled the end of my Lewis United career, as Ally MacLeod had told the junior club that he was calling me up as soon as their run in the Scottish was over.

I was told later that the Aberdeen manager's decision was not too popular with Lewis players and officials, for they were well in the running for league and cup honours and they missed me in the final run-in, eventually being pipped by Banks o' Dee for the league title. They had some consolation, however, in winning one of the cups.

As for me, any disappointment I felt over missing out on the end of the junior season was forgotten in the excitement of being called up to play in the Pittodrie reserve team.

Actually, I had made one earlier Aberdeen A appearance when Teddy Scott was short of players for a Reserve League game against Celtic A. I was listed as Trialist and played at right back.

Teddy told me later that Andy Roxburgh, then in charge of the Scotland youth squad, had been at the game and had been quite impressed with my performance, but was unable to consider me for inclusion in the national squad because he had enough defenders who were already experienced in senior clubs' reserve teams while I was still playing in junior football.

Having enjoyed my time with Lewis United, I kept up my connection with the junior club and a few years after my departure I took the team for training a couple of times. Among the players with them at the time was one by the name of Stuart Beedie, who later fulfilled the promise he showed when he moved into the senior ranks.

The transition from junior to reserve-team football on a regular basis, of course, put my game under added pressure, but that seemed to do me no harm and I soon settled down at the new level. In fact, I had some encouraging reports from Teddy Scott, who could always be relied on for a perfectly fair and frank assessment of the form of any of the youngsters in his charge.

I'll have more to say about Teddy's role at Pittodrie in a later chapter, but, for the moment, it's enough to say that he comes into the same category as 'Big Mac', the teacher I mentioned earlier — someone you could admire and respect without being in awe of him.

Needless to say, my spell in the reserve team had its setbacks, but even when I was given something of a hard time, usually when I came up against players who had had first-team experience with their clubs, I was able to benefit from it. It was all grist to the mill of my learning process.

The remainder of the 1976-77 season saw me make 21 reserve-team appearances, including three as substitute, and my next objective became a first-team outing.

That ambition was realised early in the following season, but before then we had a change of managership when Ally MacLeod left to become Scotland manager.

4

Under New Management

The departure of Ally MacLeod and the subsequent arrival at Pittodrie of Billy McNeill in June, 1977 saw the first of four managerial changeovers I have experienced in my Aberdeen career.

Billy's reign was short, but although I was essentially a reserve-team player, he seemed to take a special interest in me and my progress. Possibly as a former centre half, he had a fellow feeling for me.

The 1977-78 season brought me my first taste of first-team involvement, and although that involvement was not too extensive, it was memorable for a variety of reasons.

Willie Garner, who was later to return to Pittodrie for a spell as assistant manager during Alex Ferguson's reign, was the man standing between me and the centre-half berth in the first team, and it was a breach of discipline on Willie's part which brought me my eagerly-awaited first appearance in a competitive first-team game.

It came as an unexpected New Year present, but it was none the less welcome for coming out of the blue.

I remember being met by Billy McNeill in the corridor at Pittodrie as I arrived for training on New Year's Day.

In response to my respectful 'Happy New Year, boss', Billy said: 'Happy New Year, big man. You're playing tomorrow'.

When I got my breath back, I asked what had happened, thinking perhaps someone had been taken ill or had an accident, but all he would say was: 'Let's leave it for the moment that you're in the first team for tomorrow's game'.

Later, however, the manager explained that Willie Garner and Bobby Glennie had not observed the Hogmanay curfew that had been imposed on the first-team squad and he had decided to drop the two offenders as a disciplinary measure.

It was a brave decision, for Willie was an established first-team regular while Bobby was at that time having a first-team run. In addition, Dundee United, who were the visitors at Pittodrie the following day, were then, as now, formidable opponents. But Billy was never one to shirk the responsibilities of management, unpleasant or otherwise.

The unusual circumstances of my selection didn't make it any easier for me to sleep that night and, understandably, I was very nervous in the dressing room before the game.

The strain, however, was eased by Dave Robb, who may not have been a footballer in the Michel Platini mould, but certainly knew how to relax an anxious youngster.

Noticing my nervousness — nobody could have failed to do so — David said: 'Never mind, big Alex, if there's any time that you don't know what to do with the ball, just gie it to me!'

As it turned out, I had a reasonably good performance, didn't make any silly mistakes, and we won a dour game 1-0, thanks to a late goal by Ian Fleming.

The following day, Billy McNeill called me into his office and complimented me on my performance, but added that Willie Garner would be returning to the team for the next game.

To say I was disappointed was putting it mildly, but the manager went on to explain that he felt I was still young and inexperienced and that he didn't want to rush me, while Willie Garner, having been disciplined, was still his first-choice centre half.

So Willie and Bobby were back in the side for the next game, against Ayr United at Somerset Park, while Doug Rougvie and myself, their replacements in the New Year game, returned to the reserve team. It may have been no more than coincidence, but the Ayr game was Bobby's last appearance before being transferred to Dundee for £12,500.

Looking back, I can appreciate the wisdom of Billy McNeill's decision, but at the time it was a bitter one for me to accept.

That was my competitive debut, but I had had an earlier taste of first-team football — and it, too, held a valuable lesson for me!

One of the early pre-season friendlies Billy McNeill had arranged was against Highland League club Fraserburgh at Bellslea Park, and I was one of three substitutes used, replacing Willie Garner at centre half during the second half.

Admittedly the Aberdeen team wasn't a full-strength combine, a fair number of the 'fringe' players being included, but our new manager didn't see that as a valid excuse for the 3-0 defeat we suffered. He gave us a stiff lecture after the game on the dangers of complacency.

'I know it's a pre-season friendly with improving match fitness as the main purpose, but whenever you play a team from a lower division, it's like a cup final for them. If you take anything for granted, there's always the danger of an embarrassing result such as tonight's . . .' was the main theme of his message for us, but he probably couched it slightly more colourfully than that.

Four days later, I played in another pre-season friendly, from the start this time, against St Johnstone at Muirton Park, and we finished 3-1 winners.

But when the season proper got under way, it was back to continuing my apprenticeship in the reserve team. In fact, I had only two more first-team appearances that season — a friendly against Caledonian at Inverness in early December (we won 4-2) and the league game against Dundee United at the New Year which I've just described.

Looking up the records, I see that I made 53 reserve-team appearances in the 1977-78 season, wearing either the No 5 or No 6 jersey — and I managed to score two goals!

A player can usually judge fairly accurately how well or how badly he has played in a game, and I felt I had acquitted myself reasonably well in the few opportunities I had had in the first team, but my initial taste of action with the 'big boys' had only whetted my appetite for more.

That was to come in the following season — after *another* change of manager!

5

Under New Management — Again!

The player who looms largest in this account of my early years at Pittodrie is Willie Garner — not too surprisingly, I suppose, considering we were in contention for the same berth in the Aberdeen first team.

Anyway, it was a further misfortune befalling big Willie — breaking a leg in the first leg of our European Cup-Winners' Cup first-round tie against Marek Dimitrov in Bulgaria in mid-September — which put me back into the first team — this time on a more permanent basis — in the 1978-79 season.

By this time, we had another new manager, Alex Ferguson having succeeded Billy McNeill, who found the lure of managing Celtic, the club with whom he had won such fame as a player, too great a temptation to resist when he was offered the chance to succeed the legendary Jock Stein.

I could not, of course, suspect then that this was the beginning of an era in which the Aberdeen club would not only dispel the myth that Scottish football honours were an Old Firm preserve, but also make their presence felt on the much more prestigious European stage.

But back to my own story. When the European squad returned from Bulgaria and I learned that I was to take over from the injured Garner, a daunting — but exciting — prospect unfolded in front of me.

From my first test, against Rangers at Ibrox, we emerged with a satisfactory 1-1 draw, but any complacency this result produced was rudely dispelled a week later when in another away game we were beaten 2-1 by Hibs.

I was up against a big, awkward opponent in Tony Higgins, and with me being a raw rookie, I was given a hard time of it.

Then, on the following Wednesday, came the home leg of the European tie against Marek Dimitrov — my first taste of football at this level.

Trailing 2-3 from the first leg, Drew Jarvie and Joe Harper having scored in Bulgaria, we seemed to have a good chance of getting through and, in the event, we qualified quite comfortably with a 3-0 win at Pittodrie, Drew and Joe again finding the net after Gordon Strachan had levelled the scoring overall.

But my next European experience was less enjoyable when we travelled to West Germany and suffered a 3-0 defeat at the hands of Fortuna Düsseldorf. Winning the second leg 2-0 at Pittodrie put a better face on the performance, but it wasn't enough to keep us in the competition.

I took the Düsseldorf defeat very hard — I've always been a poor loser — but Alex Ferguson was even more dejected than I was and I remember saying 'Cheer up, boss' to him in the dressing room after the game. That was the bravery of innocence. I would certainly have hesitated before making such a remark later in my association with him.

The Düsseldorf game, however, was a lesson which would stand us in good stead later, and, in one respect at least, I found the three European games I played in that season useful.

I found that the Continental strikers were not as aggressive and didn't stick as close to me as their counterparts in domestic football did and I had more freedom to get my timing right early in the game. I think this helped me to adjust more readily to first-team football in the spell that followed.

This saw me as first-team centre half for fourteen games in succession, including three European matches, but then I was given a sharp reminder of how fortunes can fluctuate in football.

Playing in the first leg of a League Cup quarter-final against Ayr United at Somerset Park in November, I went over an ankle in the final minute of the game, which ended in a 3-3 draw.

Earlier events in a fast and furious cup tie included Steve Archibald being sent off in 55 minutes after a clash with Ayr goalkeeper Hugh Sproat, and Chic McLelland and Drew Jarvie being booked, along with two Ayr players. Ally MacLeod had returned to managing Ayr United after his ill-fated spell as Scotland manager in the World Cup finals in Argentina, and he was another to incur a booking from referee Brian McGinlay for persistently leaving the dugout to protest.

That injury wasn't my first in senior football as I'd had a couple of absences, also with ankle problems, in the reserves the season before. At that stage of my career, of course, I wasn't fully developed physically, and I think in my sudden increase in height between 15 and 17, I outgrew my strength.

After the Ayr game, we had a league game at Motherwell three days later so we stayed at Inverclyde Recreation Centre rather than make a double journey, and I remember our physiotherapist of that time, Brian Scott, having me paddling in the sea in an effort to get me fit for the Motherwell game.

The salt water treatment didn't work on that occasion, but it became a regular feature of our treatment routine, even when it meant paddling in the much colder North Sea at Aberdeen beach. Sometimes these treatment sessions ended up with three or four players having a quick 'dip' in the depths of winter. I still shiver at the thought.

I missed the Fir Park game, and Doug Rougvie, who had replaced me when I was injured at Somerset Park, retained the No 5 jersey — and kept it for the rest of the season, apart from a couple of absences through suspension.

It was February before I was back in first-team action, taking over at No 6 in a home league game against Partick Thistle when Willie Miller was suspended. A couple of games later, it was Doug Rougvie's turn for a suspension and I was back at centre half, but only for one game — a 1 - 1 draw with Celtic in a Scottish Cup quarter-final at Pittodrie. We won the replay at Celtic Park by a 2 - 1 margin, Duncan Davidson and Steve Archibald scoring our goals, but my contribution was confined to a substitute appearance when I replaced Dom Sullivan.

During my earlier injury absence, however, the lads had completed the elimination of Ayr United from the League Cup with a 3 - 1 win in the second leg at Pittodrie, and they went on to beat Hibs 1 - 0 in the semi-final at Dens Park, thanks to an extra-time goal by Stuart Kennedy.

Together with our Scottish Cup win over Celtic, this left us facing two important cup-ties at Hampden in the space of a fortnight — the League Cup final against Rangers on March 31 and a Scottish Cup semi-final against Hibs on April 11. In the event, I had only brief substitute appearances in both games, but all the same I was happy enough to be in the squad.

Inverclyde was again our base in preparation for the League Cup final and this time it was Dom Sullivan who tried paddling in the Firth of Clyde in an unsuccessful bid to recover from injury. We were joined at Largs by Mark McGhee, a £70,000 signing from Newcastle United.

Mark had an outing with the A team playing Rangers A in a deci-sive Reserve League fixture at Ibrox on the eve of the cup final, scor-ing the young Dons' only goal in a 2-1 defeat which proved to be an accurate foreshadowing of the outcome of the first-team clash the following day.

Mark played for the entire 90 minutes of the Friday night game, but as it was his first outing for three weeks because of bad weather in England, Alex Ferguson decided against having him on the bench for the final, and instead selected Neil Cooper and myself as the Hampden subs.

The big talking point of that final, of course, was the controver-sial ordering-off of Doug Rougvie following a clash with Derek John-stone, but I'm afraid I can't add much to the arguments either way because, like most others on the Aberdeen bench, I was watching the ball at the time.

But big Doug always maintained that he did nothing to the Rang-ers striker to warrant being sent off, and I have no reason to doubt the word of this honest and likeable guy.

There was also some speculation after the game over whether Bobby Clark could have averted Alex MacDonald's equalising goal in the 77th minute — Duncan Davidson, if you remember, had given us the lead 14 minutes after the interval — if he hadn't been handi-capped by an arm injury which he was trying to bring to the referee's attention when Rangers scored.

Bobby himself thought that even if he had been unhampered, he couldn't have reached the ball which took a deflection off John McMaster's heel after Alex MacDonald hit it.

I don't recall much about events following my substitution for Duncan Davidson as soon as Doug Rougvie was given his marching orders in the 83rd minute because everything passed in a blur, but I do remember being aware of an unreal atmosphere.

Apart from a couple of headers, I don't think I touched the ball, but in the third minute of the six minutes' injury time which referee Ian Foote allowed, Colin Jackson managed to evade the shackles of Steve Archibald, who had been marking him at corners, to head the winning goal.

It was a sad bus trip home to Aberdeen, naturally, but although I hated losing any game, I somehow hadn't felt really involved in that final and I was probably more cheerful than some of the older members of the team.

I could appreciate how hard it was for players such as Willie Miller, who had suffered a similar 2·1 defeat against Rangers in the Scottish Cup final a season earlier, but as far as I was concerned I had my first medal in my pocket, even though it was a runners-up and not a winners' medal.

I had also avoided a well-known affliction to which Scottish footballers are prone — first-time Hampden nerves. I hadn't been expecting to be involved in the final, and so when I was eventually thrust into the action, it happened before I could dwell on what might go wrong.

My second Hampden appearance, when we met Hibs in a Scottish Cup semi-final eleven days later, lasted longer, but only marginally so. I replaced Andy Watson in 79 minutes in Alex Ferguson's second substitution, Derek Hamilton having taken over from Chic McLelland about ten minutes after the interval.

As against Rangers, we were first to score, Steve Archibald giving us the lead in 28 minutes, but Gordon Rae equalised nine minutes later and Ally MacLeod scored the winner from the penalty spot after being brought down by Doug Rougvie just before the interval.

Between the two Hampden cup-ties, I had two full league games at centre half, a 1·0 win over Morton at Cappielow and a 0·0 home draw with Hibs only four days before we were to meet them in the semi-final. John Gardiner took over in goal for all three games while Bobby Clark recovered from his arm injury.

But when I came on as sub at Hampden, it was as a midfield player and this was to be my position for seven of the nine remaining league games of that season, because by that time Willie Garner had recovered from his broken leg and was back at centre half.

The next season — 1979-80 — was to prove a momentous one for Aberdeen, climaxing in our first Premier Division title, but that was a long away ahead when we set out in the pre-season Drybrough Cup tournament, which had been revived after a seven-year lapse.

The Drybrough Cup provided an inauspicious start to the season. We lasted only one game, Kilmarnock beating us 1·0 at Rugby Park, but it opened a new door for me.

With Willie Garner holding down the centre-half berth, I started the game on the bench, but Alex Ferguson, possibly remembering the kind of role I had played at the end of the previous season, sent me on to operate in midfield, and although the game couldn't be saved, I must have done well enough to convince him that it was worth persevering with the idea.

My defensive ability helped me as a ball-winner, and I was a fairly good passer, keeping it simple and not trying anything fancy, and the manager felt this gave a good balance alongside ball players like Gordon Strachan and John McMaster in midfield.

I undertook the midfield assignment without any great expect-ations and this allowed me to approach it in a relaxed frame of mind. In my tackling, too, I didn't feel as much responsibility resting on me as I would when playing at the back. Going into a tackle, it gives you great confidence knowing that even if you fail to get the ball, it won't be disastrous because there's a team-mate behind you as cover. In these circumstances, you can afford to commit yourself fully — and you probably win the tackle more often that not, for that very reason.

The result, anyway, was that of the fifty-odd first-team appear-ances I made that season, almost 40 were in the No 4 shirt, although I did have a run at centre half towards the end of the league pro-gramme. It was an experience I enjoyed, partly because it broad-ened the range of my skills, but also because I would have enjoyed any position which secured me a regular place in the first team.

Following on our early exit from the Drybrough Cup, the start of our league programme was equally discouraging for we lost twice away from home — to Partick Thistle and Morton — in the first four games. Morton, in fact, proved a real bogey for us that season, beat-ing us by the odd goal in each of our first three league clashes with them.

Another surprising feature of this title-winning season was that our record included four home defeats in the league. Losing at Pitto-drie to Celtic and Dundee United might not be unexpected, but for Morton and Kilmarnock to beat us there was, to say the least, unusual.

In speaking of Morton's success against us, maybe I should make it clear that it didn't extend to cup-ties, because it was the Gree-nock club we beat 2-1 at Hampden to earn a place in the League Cup final for the second year in succession.

Again, though, it was a case of so near and yet so far, and we had to be content with runners-up medals when we met Dundee United in the final in early December. We had the better of a goalless draw after extra time at Hampden, but in the replay at Dens Park, United scored a comprehensive 3-0 victory.

It was a bitter disappointment after our earlier morale-boosting triumph over Celtic, beating them in both legs of the quarter-final — 3-2 at Pittodrie, with Steve Archibald claiming a hat-trick, and 1-0 at Parkhead, where Mark McGhee was the marksman.

To get back to our league campaign, our results continued to be rather mixed and it was into the final month of the competition before serious thoughts of winning the title began to grow at Pittodrie.

In fact I can recall the exact day we began to fancy our chances — April 19. I probably remember it particularly because I missed our game with Kilmarnock at Rugby Park with a trapped nerve in my neck — which amused my room-mate John McMaster as I had to turn my whole body every time I wanted to speak to him.

I took the additional risk of watching that game from the stand, sitting next to the chairman, which, as any of his fellow-directors will confirm, can lead to treatment for injuries sustained from Mr Donald's feet as he mentally replays the on-field action in his seat, or from his discarded sweetie papers, which fly in all directions when anything goes wrong.

Anyway, we won the Kilmarnock game 3-1, and when the news filtered through at the end of the game that Celtic had been hammered 5-1 by Dundee at Dens Park, we realised that Celtic were now only two points ahead of us at the top of the table and we had a game in hand.

The buzz of excitement this caused at Pittodrie was increased four days later when we went to Celtic Park and won 3-1 to go top on goal difference and still with a game in hand.

This situation was maintained when we beat St Mirren 2-0 at Pittodrie on the Saturday, but Celtic profited from our away 1-1 draw with Dundee United in the following midweek game to edge in front again.

Then came the crunch at Easter Road on Saturday, May 3 when we beat Hibs 5-0 while Celtic, in their final fixture, had a goalless draw against St Mirren at Paisley.

This meant that with one game to go, we were in front on goal difference (which was later converted into a one-point lead by a 1-1 draw with Partick Thistle at Firhill).

Aberdeen had won their first Premier Division title and become Scottish League champions for the first time since 1955. In the next chapter, I'll try to analyse my reactions to that memorable moment in the club's history — and tell of a personal distraction I had during the celebrations.

6
Trophy Trail

If the disappointment of Aberdeen's 1978-79 League Cup final defeat was softened for me by my relative newness to the first-team squad, I was also a bit more restrained than some of my team-mates in celebrating the club's first league title win in quarter of a century in 1980.

I was just as convinced as the other players that this was the start of an important phase in the club's history, but I was still the raw youngster not quite yet fully established in the team.

I don't suppose the full significance of the event had really sunk in, whereas for the more senior players like Willie Miller, Bobby Clark and Drew Jarvie, who had waited years for this to happen, and even for the boss himself, this was the fulfilment of a long-cherished dream.

I was fresh from the juvenile ranks where I'd been accustomed to winning cup finals and league titles and it was something I had expected to continue when I joined a senior club of Aberdeen's stature. Such is the brashness of youth!

I must admit, too, that I had another, more personal, reason for not joining in the celebrations at Easter Road quite as whole-heartedly as my clubmates.

A short time before this, I had met Jill Taylor, an Aberdeen clerkess who was later to become my wife, and when I discovered that she was to be spending that weekend with an aunt and uncle who happened to live quite close to my parents' home in Glasgow, I suggested that I could have a weekend in Glasgow and we could meet.

At the time I arranged this, my first real 'date' with Jill, I didn't know, of course, that the Easter Road match would clinch the Premier Division title for us. None of us, in fact, was fully prepared for the title to be decided by that game and no arrangements had been made by the club for after-match celebrations, so everything was very much an impromptu affair.

In the event, Jill attended the Easter Road game, along with the uncle she was to be staying with in Glasgow, but I didn't discover this until later, so, after that dramatic 5-0 victory (in which, incidentally, Ian Scanlon (2), Steve Archibald, Andy Watson and Mark McGhee were the scorers), I joined the lads in the dressing-room celebrations and then went off to Glasgow with my dad, while the rest of the team made their way back to Aberdeen.

In the dressing room, we were visited by the television cameras and when *Scotsport* presenter Arthur Montford asked me how I felt about winning the Premier title, I answered: 'I'm speechless!' — and then proceeded to prove that I was anything but speechless by giving him chapter and verse about our title win.

The dressing-room scenes were quite emotional, with tears of joy from some of the lads, and I learned later that the homeward journey, too, was something special.

Stuart Kennedy, normally a total abstainer, really let his hair down that night and apparently he continued the champagne celebrations in a night club once back in Aberdeen. That was how much winning the Premier Division title meant to the Aberdeen players.

But that was just a start, the springboard for a spell in which we won nine national and two European trophies within seven seasons — the era which inspired the title of this book.

In each of these seasons, at least one trophy took up temporary residence in the Pittodrie boardroom . . . and a couple of them stayed for longer than one year.

Winning the 1979-80 Premier title was, in fact, the big breakthrough, but this wasn't immediately apparent.

At the end of that season, Scotland embarked on a short Iron Curtain tour, playing games in Poland and Hungary, and during that tour I can recall a conversation I had with Danny McGrain (who captained Scotland for the first time in the Poland game), Roy Aitken and Davie Provan.

The three Celtic players, speaking from personal experience, told me that Aberdeen would find it much harder to retain the title the following season, and although I put their remarks down to 'sour grapes' at the time, they were proved right, because in 1980-81 we had to content ourselves with finishing as runners-up — to Celtic!

But we did have an early success in winning the Drybrough Cup. There are those who would argue that a competition like this couldn't be taken as seriously as the others, and I suppose they have a case, but once you get into the final, it's just as important as any other event and you're desperate to win it.

I receive a portable colour TV set from the Association of Aberdeen FC Supporters Clubs after being voted their Player of the Year in 1984-85.

So it was with some relief that we saw Steve Cowan score the winning goal against St Mirren, a left-foot shot into the top corner of the net. After that performance, Stevie became known as 'Cup-tie' Cowan, a nickname he gets to this day from his former team-mates of that Drybrough Cup final at Hampden.

In 1981-82, we again had to give best to Celtic in the league, but we made another dent in the Old Firm domination by carrying off the Scottish Cup, beating Rangers 4-1 in the final.

We had to go into extra time to do it, but I felt we were the better team all through that final. Personally, though, that tie was particularly memorable as I scored the equalising goal which took the game into extra time. Scoring in a cup final is a great thrill even for a striker, so you can imagine how I, as a defender not noted for scoring a lot of goals, felt.

After the game, the lads were kidding me that when I scored I had been intending to cross the ball into the goalmouth, but I had the perfect answer for them as the shot which curled past Jim Stewart was almost a carbon copy of one I'd scored in training three days earlier.

As part of our cup-final preparations, we had a day at Cruden Bay, combining a training session with nine holes of golf, and it was during the morning training that I produced a rehearsal of my Hampden goal, the only difference being that the Cruden Bay one went in off the post.

To cap everything, I was selected for the 'Man of the Match' award, and the silver salver I received is among my most treasured possessions. I reckoned it was an extra honour for a defender to win it, although I suppose scoring a goal helped.

Actually I came close to scoring much earlier in the game, with a header going just over the bar, and this 'miss' made me unpopular with Scotland squadmate Alan Brazil when we met up for the end-of-season internationals the following day.

'You cost me £50, big man,' was how the Ipswich striker greeted me, and he went on to explain that he had put £5 on me at 10-1 to score the first goal of the final.

That honour, as it turned out, fell to Rangers' John MacDonald, but Alan's lost fiver apart, I was quite happy to come second on this occasion. Our extra-time goals, of course, came from Mark McGhee, Gordon Strachan and Neale Cooper.

In the 1982-83 season, the dominating feature was our European Cup-Winners' Cup triumph, but as I'll be dealing with that later, let's for the moment stick to the domestic scene.

Not for the first time — nor the last — Dundee United assumed a vital, if negative, role in our quest for honours that season. Having dealt us an early blow by beating us 2-0 at Tannadice in the opening league fixture, United then exercised their fatal fascination for us in the League Cup when they knocked us out in the quarter-final, winning both legs for a 4-1 aggregate.

We managed to turn the tables in subsequent league games, winning 5-1 at Pittodrie and 3-0 at Tannadice, but just when we were looking possible title challengers, United beat us 2-1 at Pittodrie in March.

This started a run in which we suffered three defeats in four league games, also going down 1-0 at home to St Mirren and 2-1 away to Rangers. Our league challenge was blunted and we finally had to settle for third place behind Dundee United and Celtic, with Celtic beating us on goal difference.

But there was still the Scottish Cup, and we retained the trophy, again beating Rangers in the final, this time 1-0, but the final again

Our Premier Division title-win in 1984-85 is recognised by Grampian Region.

went into extra time before Eric Black scored the all-important goal.

Having beaten Celtic 1·0 in the semi-final at Hampden a month earlier, we were looking forward to completing an Old Firm double, although it must be admitted that the final didn't occupy our minds that season as much as it normally would because ten days before our return to Hampden, we were involved in another final in Gothenburg.

Actually, I almost missed the Hampden game through injury. After returning from Gothenburg, we beat Hibs 5·0 at Pittodrie in our final league fixture, but I hurt a knee in that game and I wasn't able to train at the start of the following week. The Thursday was my dead-line, but I was still feeling pain by then and we began to discuss the possibility of playing with a painkilling injection.

By the Saturday morning, though, I was feeling pretty good after I'd given it another test. I've always had to be completely satisfied in my own mind about my fitness. If I have any doubts, I feel I can't give of my best, and on such occasions I usually go all quiet. There's none of the shouting and cajoling of my team-mates which is my usual.

Maybe it was nerves that dulled the pain, but the knee stood up to the final. Although we finally won it after extra time, we didn't play particularly well, but we still didn't expect Alex Ferguson's reaction to our performance.

I remember I remained out on the field showing off the trophy to our supporters a little longer than most of the other players, and when I finally reached the dressing room, I couldn't understand why everyone was looking so glum.

Gordon Strachan explained that the manager had been giving them stick, but it was only later when I saw the boss's after-match interview on television that I discovered, to my embarrassment, that only Willie Miller and myself of the outfield players had been let off in the manager's general condemnation of the team's display.

The players were all very disappointed, of course, but the following day, Alex Ferguson, after apologising to the players privately, admitted publicly that his attack was unwarranted, particularly in view of the Gothenburg performance only ten days earlier.

The manager's retraction, in fact, raised him in the players' estimation. They admired the bigness of a man who could admit his mistake so readily.

Another thing I remember about the 1983 Cup final was meeting Celtic's Davie Provan outside Hampden after the game and hearing his complaint about the game going into extra time. Apparently he had bet on us to win, but the bet covered only the 90 minutes of normal time.

The 1982-83 Cup double was a great experience, but we went one better in the following season by winning three major trophies — completing a hat-trick of successive Scottish Cup triumphs, winning the European Super Cup against SV Hamburg and reclaiming the elusive Premier Division title with a new record tally of 57 points.

The league triumph, we felt, was particularly significant, for after winning the Cup-Winners' Cup a season earlier, the club's sights were now set on the European Champions' Cup and this meant winning the Premier Division title to earn qualification for the top European event.

Setting a new points record was satisfying, but the defenders took even greater pleasure from our 'goals against' figure of 21 — a new record — and even that might have been lower if we hadn't conceded three goals in our final fixture, away to St Mirren. This was our first defeat in eleven league games and only the fourth in thirty-six Premier games that season.

The Love Street game was just a week before we were due to face

Celtic in the Scottish Cup final and the boss decided to rest some of the regulars — Gordon Strachan, Peter Weir, Willie Miller and myself.

Over the years, Willie Miller, Jim Leighton and myself developed quite an understanding of each other's play, and together with the other defenders, who changed more frequently, we took just as much pride in preventing the opposition from scoring as our strikers took in putting the ball in the opposition's net. After a game we would discuss and analyse the goals we had lost, working out where we had gone wrong, so that we wouldn't make the same mistake again.

That season, we had kept the against-goals tally down to 18 in the first 35 league games, keeping the opposition scoresheet blank in 21 of these games, but a fairly young Aberdeen team went down 3-2 at Love Street, with Frank McDougall, who was later to join us at Pittodrie, claiming Saints' opening goal.

An earlier meeting with St Mirren, at Pittodrie in March, had given us double cause for celebration. A 2-0 win saw us equal a four-year-old record run of twenty-seven competitive games without defeat (a 2-0 defeat against Ujpest Dozsa in Hungary in the next game prevented us breaking the record), while Gordon Strachan's penalty conversion to open the score gave him his 100th goal for the club.

In the '83-84 Scottish Cup final, we had to go into extra time for the third year in succession to complete our hat-trick of trophy wins in this event with a 2-1 victory over Celtic. My international squad-mate Roy Aitken achieved an unenviable distinction in this final when he became the first player to be ordered off in a Scottish Cup final. The dismissal of the Celtic captain, for a heavy tackle on Mark McGhee, should have made our task easier, but, as so often happens, the ten-man Celtic side fought even harder while I suppose we probably became a bit complacent, thinking we could just stroll to victory after Eric Black put us in front with a characteristic goal from a setpiece situation.

The boss gave us a thorough going-over at half-time, and again on the touchline after 90 minutes, by which time Celtic had forced the tie into extra time through an equaliser by Paul McStay. His words must have had some effect because we were more like ourselves in extra time. Our luck seemed to be out when a great shot by Doug Bell struck the woodwork, but the ball was only cleared to Gordon Strachan, who crossed for Mark McGhee to net the winner.

This win over Celtic avenged our earlier dismissal from the

League Cup when we were beaten 1·0 on aggregate by the Parkhead club at the semi-final stage.

The following season — 1984-85 — was less successful, but we still took the most-prized trophy in retaining the Premier Division title, pushing the points record two notches higher with a final tally of 59 points.

In other domestic competition, we suffered a humiliating 3·1 defeat against Airdrie at Broomfield in the second round of the Skol League Cup, and went out to Dundee United at the semi-final stage of the Scottish Cup. Our three-year grip on the trophy ended at Tynecastle when United won 2·1 in a replay, the first meeting at the same ground producing no goals.

The Tannadice side were also responsible that season for ending our record run of twenty-four home Premier Division games undefeated when they scored a 1·0 victory at Pittodrie three days before Christmas.

In the later stages of the league programme, I was getting a hard time from Willie Miller because I hadn't scored in a competitive game that season. Willie and I usually have our own private scoring competition, which has the beauty that it isn't too difficult to calculate our respective tallies, but we both argue that it's the quality rather than the quantity of goals which counts!

On this occasion, I had scored in one of the pre-season friendlies in West Germany, but that scarcely counted, and Willie was making the most of having a couple of league goals to his credit while I had none. You can imagine my delight when in the fourth-last fixture I scored the opening goal in a 4·0 win over Dumbarton. But Willie had the last laugh, because he scored the vital goal which gave us a 1·1 draw with Celtic at Pittodrie in the very next game to bring his season's goal tally to three.

For Willie and me, though, scoring goals was the icing on the cake. Our principal concern was preventing them, and anything we can contribute at the other end is incidental to having a good season, as someone like Alan Hansen proves season after season without figuring among Liverpool's leading scorers.

Actually, I regard '84-85 as one of my best seasons at Pittodrie, and many of the Dons' fans must have agreed with me, because I received the Association of Aberdeen FC Supporters' Clubs award that season.

My solitary league goal was a heaven-sent opportunity for the

The Dons' squad accept the plaudits of the crowd after completing the league and Scottish Cup double in Season 1983-84.

manager to wind me up, until I made the point that my goal against Dumbarton took our tally for competitive games that season to the hundred mark. Strictly speaking, that wasn't completely accurate, because although we did pass the century mark in that game, it was the third goal, scored by Billy Stark, and not mine, which clocked up the 100. The boss didn't argue, though.

Back to my story. A notable omission from the list of trophies we had been winning regularly in the early '80s had been the League Cup, and people were beginning to wonder if this was one title which was going to evade Alex Ferguson. That idea, though, was eventually dispelled in the 1985-86 season when we triumphed in the Skol League Cup, as it had become by then, and collected two trophies — the sponsors' Skol Cup and the League Cup itself — after beating Hibs 3-0 in the final at Hampden in October.

This was the first of two successful visits we made to the national stadium that season. We returned there in the Scottish Cup final in May to complete a 'capital' double, if you'll excuse the pun, by recording a similar-margin win over Hearts.

These two finals differed from earlier Hampden visits in that we didn't need extra time, but they shared one common feature, apart from the home city of our opponents. Billy Stark, in my view one of Alex Ferguson's best acquisitions for Aberdeen, but a player who was more appreciated by his team-mates than by most of the club's supporters, scored in both games, with Eric Black contributing the other two goals against Hibs and John Hewitt performing a similar feat against Hearts.

Billy's value was underlined during our league campaign that season when he scored his 50th goal in his 107th first-team appearance — a more-than-useful average for a midfield player!

And John Hewitt's contribution to our Scottish Cup win was very much in keeping with the tremendous cup-tie form he had shown that season when he always seemed to be collecting the man-of-the-match awards.

Mention of the 1986 Scottish Cup final reminds me that it could well have turned into a nightmare for yours truly — because I had to play in borrowed boots!

When the kit was unpacked at Hampden, it was discovered that the boots marked A. McL. weren't mine, but belonged to reserve striker Andy McLeod, who was the same initials as myself, but wears size $7\frac{1}{2}$ in boots to my $9\frac{1}{2}$.

With the kick-off little more than an hour away, it was impossible to get new boats, but the ever-resourceful Teddy Scott came to my rescue by 'doctoring' Bryan Gunn's size $10\frac{1}{2}$ boots (or boats, some might say) to fit me. Teddy padded them at the heel and I wore two pairs of socks to fill up the extra space.

Well-fitting and comfortable boots are a top priority with most footballers, but, fortunately, my strange footwear didn't put me off. In fact, on one occasion in the second half when I joined in an attack, I managed to switch play with a long pass to the other wing which found a team-mate. Big Ben Gunn later claimed that pass as a success for his boots.

Our '85-86 Premier Division challenge, to be frank, was a big disappointment and we could do no better than a fourth-place finish. Our failure to complete a league hat-trick, I think, led to sections of the Press writing us off as having an indifferent season, but we felt that winning two cups wasn't too bad for an indifferent season.

7

Europe : The Ups and Downs

European football, by its very nature, is a powerful stimulant. The very thought of playing on such a huge stage is enough to set the professional footballer's pulses racing and the adrenalin flowing.

For me, though, the European cup encounters stir memories of moments of great sadness as well as great joy.

Nothing could be higher than the 'high' experienced when Aberdeen won the European Cup-Winners' Cup final in Gothenburg in May, 1983 (with the possible exception of winning the European Champions' Cup), but equally sharp, at the other end of the scale,

The Dons' squad prepare to leave Aberdeen Airport during their 1987-88 UEFA Cup campaign.

was the 'low' I went through while abroad on European business in December, 1981, when I was informed of my father's sudden death.

I was very close to my dad and consider him to have been a major influence on my football career. We were in West Germany for the second leg of a UEFA Cup third-round tie against SV Hamburg, and we'd just been beaten 3-1 for a 5-4 losing aggregate when the news was broken to me in a phone call from my wife Jill.

My father had died early the previous day, but as there was nothing I could have done immediately, it was decided to keep the news from me until after the game.

Injury had kept me out of the first leg of that tie and I made my comeback only on the Saturday before the second leg when we played Morton at Cappielow. I met my father at Greenock and he told me that he was going back to his work on the following Monday for the first time since having a heart attack four months earlier.

Apparently his doctor wanted him to stay off work a little longer, but dad was the type who couldn't bear being idle and he felt strong enough to return.

Our journey home from Hamburg seemed to me to go on forever, and I kept thinking about things my dad had said to me over the years, and how he had always been the severest, yet most helpful, critic of my play.

When I played my full international debut, for instance, my performance drew quite a lot of praise in the newspapers, but dad's approval was tempered by the observation that I 'seemed to tire in the second half'.

That was the kind of support he gave, always nudging me on to improve in one way or another. Sensing how much I was going to miss my father's influence, Alex Ferguson assured me that he would take my dad's place as much as he could in keeping me up to scratch. That was an assurance I was glad of, both then and in later years.

Between the 'low' of my father's death and the 'high' of Gothenburg, there lay only seventeen months, or eleven games in terms of European ties, but in reality our progress to a European title had started some time before the Hamburg games.

Some might even date the commencement of our European apprenticeship back to our European Cup debut in 1980-81 when, after a solid performance in accounting for Austria Memphis in the

The Aberdeen squad leaving for Gothenburg give special treatment to the singing telegram girl who gave them a good luck message from their wives. Willie Miller is so relaxed, he's just about asleep.

first round, holding out for a goalless draw in Vienna after a 1·0 win at Pittodrie, we were given a sharp lesson in what European football was all about by masters of that particular art. Liverpool became only the third team to win a European tie at Pittodrie when they beat us 1·0 there, and followed up with a 4·0 victory at Anfield.

But I think that the first positive step we took towards our eventual Cup-Winners' Cup triumph was in the following season when we started our UEFA Cup campaign by claiming the scalp of Ipswich, who were defending champions in the event.

In preparing for the first leg of that tie at Portman Road, I was expecting to have to contend with Paul Mariner, who was also the England No 9 at that time, but he was ruled out by injury at the last minute and this meant a slight revision of our defensive plans.

We gave a great display in holding Ipswich to a 1·1 draw, yours truly having a hand in the goal, scored by John Hewitt, following a corner kick.

Any fears our supporters might have had of a letdown at Pittodrie in the second leg were quickly dispelled. We took the English team to pieces before finishing winners by a 3-1 margin which could have been wider. Gordon Strachan, who scored with a 19th-minute penalty which was later equalised by John Wark, also from the penalty spot, had a twice-taken penalty kick saved by Paul Cooper at the second attempt in injury time after Peter Weir had scored two second-half goals.

Knocking out the UEFA Cup-holders so emphatically lifted Aberdeen almost overnight from the 'unknowns' of European football, but remaining in the ranks of rated clubs was another matter. Our emergence from obscurity, in fact, almost became a temporary affair in the second round when our European education was further enlarged with a trip behind the Iron Curtain to face Arges Pitesti in Romania.

Holding a 3-0 lead from the first leg at Pittodrie, complacency was always a threat and the roof seemed likely to cave in when the Romanians led 2-0 at the interval in the second leg.

This led to what might be termed Alex Ferguson's 'Tea Cup Talk-In' when, as Gordon Strachan so graphically described in his autobiography, items of crockery and the tea urn — accidentally? — went flying in different directions in our dressing room as the manager tried to impress on us the error of our ways in that first half.

The second half saw us go out determined to prove the boss wrong, and goals scored by Gordon (from the penalty spot) and John Hewitt earned a 2-2 draw and a 5-2 winning aggregate.

But the harsh lesson we narrowly avoided having inflicted on us in Romania was only delayed until our third-round meeting with SV Hamburg.

I suppose the West German side, which included the legendary Franz Beckenbauer, were just too experienced as European campaigners for us, but we contributed to our own downfall by throwing away overall victory with mistakes in the first leg at Pittodrie.

Strangely enough, that game also featured a penalty miss for Gordon Strachan. Eric Black, making his European debut, gave us a 23rd-minute lead, but Hamburg equalised before the interval, and between the goals Andy Watson and John Hewitt scored in the second half, Gordon had his spot-kick effort saved.

Our inexperience showed when, following an injury to Doug

The Aberdeen squad board their plane bound for Gothenburg.

Rougvie, Hamburg scored a second goal, taking advantage of Aberdeen being momentarily reduced to ten men before Neale Cooper could be brought on as substitute.

In Hamburg, the Germans established a 3-0 lead before Mark McGhee, appearing as a second-half substitute, scoring a consolation goal, but, for me, the disappointment of that defeat was swallowed up by the news of my father's death.

Little did we think as we started our 1982-83 Cup-Winners' Cup campaign with a preliminary-round tie against little-known FC Sion that we would go all the way this time and land the title, but the indications were there all the way through a series of competent performances.

The Swiss tie was little more than two gentle warm-up games — 7-0 at Pittodrie and 4-1 at Sion — against a side who were to gain sweet revenge by putting us out by a 4-2 aggregate in the first round of the same competition four years later.

The first round of the competition proper was to see us in the rather outlandish surroundings of Albania where we held Dinamo Tirana to a goalless draw after a 1-0 win at Pittodrie.

We had heard of Albania's determination to isolate itself from the rest of Europe, and the place itself certainly lived up to its reputation. Communication in particular was extremely uncertain and this, in fact, resulted in folk back home in Scotland believing briefly that the country had been plunged into a political uprising at the time we were there.

The so-called 'attempted coup' — which had actually occurred two days before we even arrived in the country — had amounted to no more than a suicidal attempt by four armed pro-Royalists to land on a beach fifty miles from the capital, resulting in three of them being killed and the fourth captured.

We learned later that the concern which reports of the incident caused at home was increased by the fact that it was apparently impossible to contact our hotel to establish what had happened.

Doubts over the quality of the food in Albania had led to us taking in huge stocks of Mars bars, etc, but fears that we wouldn't be able to eat what was served up proved ill-founded.

But not the stories we had heard about the strictness of the Customs regulations. Several of us, for example, had British newspapers confiscated on our arrival simply because the page 3 picture was against regulations. Noticing that the offending papers were not destroyed, but carefully filed away in a drawer, we wondered if the officials kept them for their own secret enjoyment, but this theory was discounted by the punctilious return of the material on our departure, with a receipt having to be signed for its safe return.

On our way home, we had visions of having to leave Stuart Kennedy in Albania. Our departure was delayed for almost an hour while Stuart tried to explain why he was leaving the country with more money than he had arrived with. He had quite a job convincing the authorities that the extra cash — it amounted to only a few pounds — was the proceeds of a successful card session with his team-mates, and not, as they obviously thought, the product of dealings in the local currency black market.

Our good form continued in the second round when we beat Lech Poznan at Pittodrie and 1-0 in Poland, but better was to follow in the quarter-finals when for the first time that season we were drawn against highly-rated opposition in Bayern Munich, and with the first leg away from home.

Wet but happy, the Aberdeen squad gather round the cup on the Gothenburg pitch.

The Bayern side at that time included such household names as Karl Heinz Rumenigge and Paul Breitner. It almost seemed as if it was written into the Bayern players' contracts that they had to pass to Breitner, such was the deference paid to the international midfield general.

A description of our visit to Munich demands a couple of superlatives. Holding Bayern to a goalless draw was probably Aberdeen's best-ever away performance in Europe, while the Olympic Stadium in Munich was certainly the best football pitch I've ever played on, or, for that matter, seen.

It was a fantastic stadium and I remember Archie Knox saying when we made our usual eve-of-match visit to the ground: 'If ye canna play on this pitch, ye canna play fitba.'

In my juvenile days in Glasgow where red ash pitches were the norm, we regarded it as a luxury to play on a grass pitch. The same applied to the Olympic Stadium when compared to normal grass pitches. It positively gave you a thrill to step on the pitch and after seeing it, the boys couldn't wait to get out and play on it.

We played really well that night and it was a performance-and-a-half by Dougie Bell, who was having a terrific season. With the Germans desperate to get a goal in the later stages, all we had to do was give the ball to Dougie, who would set out on one of his mazy runs and keep the ball for several minutes at a time.

After the game, though, the boss made sure that our success didn't go to our heads. He warned us that the Germans would be a lot more dangerous when they came to Pittodrie than they had been in the first leg, and he reinforced this warning by imposing fines on some of the players who went out for a celebratory drink that night without obtaining his permission first.

For the return leg, we based our tactics on what was by then our normal pattern for home European ties — whirlwind, typically Scottish football to which the Continentals were not accustomed. As the boss and Archie kept preaching: 'Play the game the way they don't want it played. They like to play it slow, but don't let them. Get at them fast and close them down early'.

We started reasonably well, but, following a Breitner free kick, Augenthaler scored for Bayern. Neil Simpson equalised before the interval after an Eric Black header had been blocked on the goal line, but that still left Bayern with the advantage on the away goals rule, and it looked very black for us when Bayern went ahead again.

That was when John McMaster and Gordon Strachan produced their well-rehearsed 'double act' in which they appeared to get in each other's way in taking a free kick. On this occasion, the con trick worked to perfection.

The Bayern defence were thrown off guard as both players turned away, apparently in disgust over the mix-up, but Gordon quickly turned back and took the free kick and I was able to get my head to the ball and send it into the net. It was the only goal I have — so far — scored in Europe, but it's one I'll never forget. Even after the game, the Germans remained convinced that the little act between Gordon and John had been a genuine mix-up and not a well-rehearsed manoeuvre.

At 2-2, the Germans were still favourites to go through, but only a minute later John Hewitt, living up to the super-sub tag which he came to hate, but which he certainly earned that season, scored the winning goal after Eric Black had had another attempt blocked.

Jubilation as we congratulate John Hewitt scoring the winner against Bayern Munich, in the Cup Winners' Cup quarter-final second leg at Pittodrie (1982-83).

For once, I was in no hurry to get home to Westhill after a game. I felt I wanted to stay and mingle with the fans, and along with an uncle and some friends, I spent an enjoyable time reliving the game with the regulars in a city pub I sometimes went to.

We were in a European semi-final for the first time and, having accounted for triple former European Cup-winners in Bayern, we feared none of our remaining opponents — Waterschei, Austria Vienna and the legendary Real Madrid.

It was the Belgian club who came out of the hat as our semi-final opponents, and using our whirlwind tactics to good effect, we virtually assured ourselves of a place in the final by winning the first leg at Pittodrie by a 5-1 margin.

That game, incidentally, was my 250th first-team appearance for Aberdeen, and by a strange coincidence, my 500th also came in a European game — the first leg of our UEFA Cup first-round tie against Bohemians in Dublin last season.

We were in dazzling form in that 5-1 win with Mark McGhee (2), Eric Black, Neil Simpson and Peter Weir claiming the goals, but it was again Dougie Bell who shone brightest. Apparently, though, not everyone shared our confidence about the second leg. On meeting a regular Aberdeen supporter outside Pittodrie the following day, I was greeted with: 'That was some result last night, but don't you think that away goal could be costly?'

In the event, the second leg against Waterschei brought our only disappointment — and only defeat — of that campaign when the Belgian side won 1-0.

Injuries sustained in the Scottish Cup semi-final victory over Celtic three days earlier ruled out four first-choice players for the game in Genk, but it was a simple defensive mistake, both Willie Miller and myself slipping at the same time, which cost us the decisive goal.

More seriously in the long term, Stuart Kennedy suffered a knee injury when his studs caught in the ground and cost him a place in the final and eventually led to him having to give up the game altogether. On the brighter side, that game saw Willie Falconer — only a few days past his 17th birthday — make his European debut when he appeared as a second-half substitute.

But the strangest feature of the Waterschei game was the air of depression which settled over the players in the dressing room afterwards. The fact that we were safely in the final seemed to be forgotten in the disappointment we felt over losing our unbeaten record.

I clash with Eurice of Porto in our Cup-Winners' Cup semi-final (1983-84).

Even the boss commented on this during the after-match dinner. In the course of his speech he said that it was an indication of how far we had come that losing the one game should produce such disappointment.

It wasn't all gloom, though, and at least one of our number retained his sense of humour. We had each received a gift of a box of strawberries from the hospitable Belgians and this prompted the crack: 'At least they didn't give us raspberries!'

You might think that a big event like the Cup-Winners' Cup final should have a chapter to itself, but that historic game in the Ullevi Stadium on May 11, 1983 has been gone over so many times that I'll just give some personal reflections on what went on behind the scenes in Gothenburg and how the players felt about this unforgettable event.

Alex Ferguson was determined to keep our preparations for the meeting with Real Madrid as normal as possible, but for me, they were different in at least one respect. I spent the two nights before the game sleeping on the floor of my hotel bedroom!

A few days earlier I had hurt my back lifting some paving stones at my home in Westhill — I was told later by the workmen that they were too heavy for lifting single-handed and I should have moved them some other way — and although the massage treatment I was getting from physiotherapist Roland Arnott was helping, I was still feeling uncomfortable in bed. I tried putting a wooden board under the mattress, but finally found it most comfortable lying on the floor covered by a quilt.

Our hotel was a few miles outside Gothenburg in a village called Farshatt — a name which inevitably prompted jokes when spoken in an Aberdeenshire accent — and the quietness was perfect for our purpose. To keep our minds off the coming game, the boss had organised a team quiz and this was conducted amid a great deal of banter and bending of the rules.

This was another example of the manager's thoroughness of approach, which included inviting Jock Stein to accompany the team to Gothenburg in case there was anything the Scotland manager, from his vast experience of European cup football, could suggest which the boss himself might have overlooked. SFA secretary Ernie Walker was also with the party to help with any administrative problems which might arise.

Our training session at the Ullevi Stadium the day before the game attracted more Press and media people than I've ever seen before on these occasions and the glorious weather gave us no indication of the incessant rain of the following day.

The rain was so heavy that we wondered if the game might have to be postponed, but that happens only very rarely with a European final. But the weather did have an influence on the game, and my contribution to it in particular.

Action from the Cup-Winners' Cup (1983-84) quarter-final (second leg) against Ujpest Dozsa at Pittodrie.

Before the kick-off, I was very conscious of the need to give passes more air than usual because of the rain-soaked pitch, but that pre-match resolve was momentarily forgotten in the 14th minute when I instinctively sent the ball back to Jim Leighton ALONG THE GROUND, and it was, of course, held up by the wet turf, allowing Santillana to nip in and get a penalty when Jim brought him down.

To this day, I kid Jim that the penalty was his fault because he was slow in coming off his line, but it was clearly me forgetting about the ground conditions which was to blame for Juanito getting the opportunity to equalise with a spot kick.

This came after we had made a dream start with Eric Black, having sent a volley against the crossbar in the third minute, putting us into the lead three minutes later with a close-range shot after I had made a late run to head in a Gordon Strachan flag kick — just one of the many times we had successfully used this setpiece manoeuvre on the big occasion.

I felt terrible over the equaliser, but fortunately it didn't upset my concentration as much as it might have done. Any feelings of guilt I may have had were finally banished when the boss went out of his way after the game to compliment me on the way I had handled the situation. That praise meant a lot to me that night and later I was able to claim that I had 'made' two goals in a European final.

Over the first 90 minutes of the final, I felt we were the better side, but it wasn't until Peter Weir, Mark McGhee and John Hewitt combined to produce that unforgettable winning goal in the 21st minute of extra time that I was relieved of the burden of my early mistake. Before the winner came, Real seemed happy to play out time and await the penalty-kick session, but that was something we didn't fancy. I certainly didn't: I was one of the players nominated as a penalty-taker.

The strain of the last few minutes of extra time could be gauged by our players' reaction when a twice-taken free kick by Salguere rocketed just wide of goal in the closing minute. An incident which in normal circumstances would maybe have brought a sigh of relief was followed on this occasion by a roar from the Aberdeen players as if we had scored another goal.

The after-match celebrations in the team hotel are now something of a pleasurable blur in my memory, but not, I hasten to add, because of over-indulgence in celebratory drinks. In fact, our intake of alcohol that night was very moderate, and this was only partly due to our professionalism, knowing that we had a game on the Saturday. For all the lads, this was the highspot of their respective football careers, and they wanted to savour the experience to the full. They didn't need any artificial stimulant to enjoy the occasion.

It was a long night, but there was a lot more celebrating still to come the next day on our return to an overwhelming reception from the city of Aberdeen — and I mean the whole city! In fact that was a feature of the congratulations that flooded in for the next couple of days. The whole of Scotland, and particularly the North-East corner of it, was revelling in our triumph, whether or not they knew the difference between a football and a rugby ball.

On the flight home, the pilot warned us that the streets of Aberdeen were lined waiting for our arrival, but the number of people who turned out was simply unbelievable. It took us hours to complete the relatively short journey in an open-topped bus from the airport to Pittodrie where the welcome home continued for another hour or so.

Later, at home, there were messages of congratulation from far and near to be opened, and I was particularly touched by 'Welcome home, Alex' cards specially made by the pupils of the local primary school.

That was a couple of days we wanted to go on forever, but the celebrations had to end some time and by the Thursday night, I suppose, we were all emotionally drained and ready to get back to near-normality with training on Friday in preparation for the Saturday game against Hibs at Pittodrie, and the Scottish Cup final against Rangers at Hampden a week later.

After the 'high' of the past few days, most of us, I think, suffered the reaction of a brief 'low' as we tried to readjust ourselves to everyday life.

There was, of course, a postscript to the Cup-Winners' Cup triumph six months later when we captured the European Super Cup by beating our former adversaries and Champions' Cup-winners, SV Hamburg.

Although in theory this should have been a more difficult and therefore a more prestigious achievement, it actually proved to be almost an anti-climax after Gothenburg.

We went to Hamburg for the first leg in late November and drew 0-0. By this time we were beginning to develop a kind of arrogance towards these occasions, which was exactly what the manager wanted so that we could go to these places and get a favourable result. Apart from the odd flurry of pressure, Hamburg never really threatened us in the first leg and we actually created more chances than the home side.

The Germans came to Pittodrie a month later, having completed a Far East tour during the mid-season break, and after a goalless first half, we dominated the second and won comfortably with goals from Neil Simpson and Mark McGhee, with Hamburg apparently resigned to defeat long before the end.

8

To Cap It All

On the international football field, I have served under three Scotland managers, four if you include Ally MacLeod, who first gave me international recognition during his brief spell in charge of the national team.

But that was in the Under-21 squad and Jock Stein had succeeded Ally as Scotland manager before I made my full international debut in a rearranged European championship qualifying match against Portugal at Hampden Park on March 26, 1980.

That my first Under-21 selection came as a pleasant surprise is an understatement. I was only a couple of weeks past my 19th birthday at the time, and, more unusually, I was still basically a reserve-team player at Pittodrie.

When manager MacLeod, having named a sixteen-strong squad to meet the Welsh Under-21s at Wrexham on February 7, 1978, experienced one of those mass withdrawals to which all Scotland managers have been subject from time to time, he must have recalled something in my favour from his spell as Aberdeen manager, when I had been one of his signings from the juvenile ranks.

On this occasion, no fewer than seven players — including Aberdeen's Stuart Kennedy, who had been one of the over-age players — had withdrawn due mainly to their clubs being involved in rearranged Scottish cup-ties, and I was one of six replacements named, another being Davie Dodds of Dundee United.

We were beaten 1-0, but when, after the game, I expressed disappointment with the result, I remember Ally telling me: 'Aye, but there are more important things than results at this level', so I suppose he was pleased with my performance.

This impression seemed to be confirmed when I became a regular member of the Under-21 squad for the next couple of years, not always getting a game, and sometimes not even a place on the bench, but nearly always named in the pool.

Further evidence that I had 'arrived' on the international scene

The Aberdeen contingent in the Scotland squad for the World Cup qualifying match against Australia in Melbourne in December, 1985.

came in December, 1979 when we played Belgium at Tynecastle in a European Under-21 championship fixture which had been postponed by bad weather ten months earlier. At that time I was playing in midfield for Aberdeen and it was this role I was given for the Under-21s.

The game finished in a 2-2 draw, but I must have impressed someone for I learned later that Anderlecht had made a £200,000 offer for me. But neither I nor the Aberdeen club were interested in parting company with each other.

Other Under-21 squad members of that period who are still going strong included Roy Aitken (with whom I was to form a lasting friendship in the senior squad at a later date), John Wark, Gary Gillespie, Eamonn Bannon, George McCluskey, Ally Dawson, Brian Whittaker and Billy Thomson, while among the over-age players were Pittodrie clubmates Steve Archibald and Gordon Strachan and the vastly entertaining Andy Ritchie of Morton.

We went on to the quarter-finals of the championship — something which the Scotland senior squad consistently failed to do — and came very close to accounting for old enemies England. In the first leg at Coventry, a strong England side which included players such as Garth Crooks and Cyrille Regis gained a 2-1 victory, Steve Archibald scoring our goal.

My old schoolmate Peter Weir, who was with St Mirren at this time, was included in the squad for the return leg at Pittodrie a fortnight later, but had to withdraw through injury, as had Gordon Strachan, one of three over-age players named, and with Celtic players being excluded because of a club commitment, the side wasn't as strong as it might have been.

Despite tremendous support from a full house at Pittodrie, we couldn't snatch the one goal we needed to go through and had to content ourselves with a goalless draw.

This game, on March 4, 1980, was my last Under-21 appearance until I returned as over-age player and captain almost seven years later. Three weeks after playing against England Under-21s, I was to make my full international debut, but, as with my entry into the Under-21 squad, my promotion came out of the blue.

The European championship match against Portugal, which was due at Hampden in early February, had been postponed by snow and was rearranged for late March. I was pleasantly surprised to find myself joining clubmates Willie Miller and Steve Archibald when a recast squad was announced, but I didn't expect to be in action at this early stage. Simply to be in the squad was a step-up, and an encouraging one at a time when Jock Stein was rebuilding the side for the next World Cup campaign.

In fact, joining the senior squad for the first time was an additional excitement, because that same weekend I attended the Scottish Professional Footballers' Association annual dinner where I was in the running for both the Player of the Year and Young Player of the Year awards. My disappointment over being pipped by John MacDonald of Rangers for the Young Player honour by the margin of a single vote — after a recount — was keen, but short-lived, thanks to a comment by Scotland manager Jock Stein.

Commiserating with me on missing the Young Player award so narrowly, he said: 'Don't worry about it, son. Get back to your hotel and get plenty of rest for Wednesday'.

Mexico 1986. Roy Aitken, myself, Willie Miller and Gordon Strachan have a day at the races during the World Cup preparations in Santa Fe, New Mexico, USA.

This raised my hopes of playing against Portugal, and sure enough, although, for once, there were no withdrawals from the squad, I was named in the starting line-up. With Dave Narey and Alan Hansen as the central defenders, I had a midfield role along with Archie Gemmill and Graeme Souness.

From the European championship viewpoint, the Hampden match had little significance as both Portugal and ourselves were out of the running for a place in the finals, but that mattered little to me, and to complete a memorable occasion, I had a good game as we won 4·1, with Kenny Dalglish, Andy Gray, Steve Archibald and Archie Gemmill (penalty) providing the Scottish goals.

As I mentioned before, my father brought me down to earth after the game by asking me if I tired in the second half, but I understood his motives for the put-down and I wasn't downhearted for long. I felt my full international career was on its way, and this was confirmed subsequently. The Portugal match started a series in which I missed only two isolated games in fifteen internationals. Later in my career, between May 1983 and December 1985, I played in twenty-three successive internationals, the last fourteen of these in an unbroken central defensive partnership with Willie Miller.

In my more fanciful moments, I sometimes reflect on the opportunity which international football gave me of becoming, would you believe it, a film star. Seriously, though, I did once have the chance of making some 'extra' money in films.

It came when Scotland went on an end-of-season tour to play Poland and Hungary a couple of months after the Portugal game. At that time, a film called *Escape to Victory,* starring Sylvester Stallone and Michael Caine and telling the story of a POW escape attempt centred round a football match, was being shot in Hungary. Jock Stein said that any of us who wanted could stay on after the tour game as the film-makers were looking for extras for the football scenes in the Nep Stadium.

Pele, Ossie Ardiles, Bobby Moore and Mike Summerbee were among the top-class footballers who took part and John Wark actually had a small speaking part. The idea quite appealed to me, but at that time I had just started dating Jill, and getting home proved a stronger magnet.

But whenever I see that film nowadays, I wonder whether it could have been enhanced by the appearance of a certain red-headed Scotsman. Such are the dreams of fame and fortune!

That was my first experience of an international tour and it gave me an insight into why Scotland team managers place such value on these occasions. Having all the squad together over an extended period is so much more effective for improving teamwork and team spirit than the couple of days which is all that is possible for clubs to release players for an individual international during the season.

For the players, too, a tour provides an opportunity to get to know the players from other clubs really well on a friendly basis which isn't possible when meeting them in competition. That Poland-Hungary tour, for example, dispelled stories I had heard about the Anglo-Scottish players being big-headed and aloof. It was great to find out that players like wee Archie Gemmill were just like ourselves and had no superior airs about them.

Mention of Anglos leads me on to a particular international fixture which means something special to most Scottish players — the annual match with the Aul' Enemy.

The broadening of international horizons, through World Cup and European championship qualifying campaigns, may in recent

The Scotland Under-21 squad who faced England at Coventry in February, 1980.

years have devalued this, the oldest international fixture in the world, but in many ways it's still a unique occasion and one to be savoured.

Of the half-dozen or so Scotland-England games I've played in, the ones I remember best are the first two — and for different reasons.

Disappointment was my chief emotion after the game at Hampden in May, 1980, not so much because England won 2-0 as because I wasn't happy with my own contribution.

I was still operating as a midfield player at that time with Willie Miller teamed up with Paul Hegarty in central defence. Emlyn Hughes was playing at the back for England that day and he used his vast experience to handle anything we could produce, which, frankly, wasn't very much.

I ended up feeling the game had passed me by, so little did I contribute, and I could scarcely argue with my father's after-match comment that I didn't even manage to kick anybody, which was his way of saying that I would have been better employed by becoming more involved, even if it was only man-marking one of the English side out of the game and leaving someone else to do the creative work.

But it was a different story at Wembley the following year. We

secured a victory — never an easy feat at Wembley — albeit by only a
1·0 margin, thanks to a John Robertson penalty goal, but the greatest satisfaction was that the whole team played well.

I was back in defence and up against big Peter Withe and felt I did
OK, but it was my partner Willie Miller who took the top defensive
honours. I reckon that was the first time Willie received full credit
from the Press for his performances, and I'll have much more to say
on this topic in a later chapter.

I've never experienced stomach butterflies to the extent I did
when I walked out of the tunnel on to the famous Wembley pitch. It
may have been England's home game, but there were Lion Ram-
pants everywhere around the ground. I remember looking up at the
stand, trying to pick out my dad, and although I was unsuccessful, I
did have the encouragement of seeing one familiar face, a chap who
lived only a few doors away from my parents' home in Barrhead.

At that time our names were not too familiar to some of the com-
mentators and I was told that one — I think it was Laurie McMenemy
— referred to Willie and myself as 'the sweeper and the big ginger-
headed fellow'.

By the end of the game, we were all feeling the physical effects of
playing on the huge and lush Wembley pitch, but I was completely
happy as I left the pitch after the game, arm-in-arm with Willie and
with a Wembley victory to savour.

The final stages of two World Cup competitions, obviously, were
milestones in my international career, but with Allan Evans as Jock
Stein's first choice at that time, my playing contribution in Spain in
1982 was limited to a substitute appearance for the final 20 minutes
against Brazil in Seville.

When I went on in place of Asa Hartford, the Brazilians were
already assured of victory, the surprise early lead Scotland had
taken through Dave Narey having been overtaken by three goals
from the South American wizards.

Actually, the two things I remember most vividly of that occasion
were not directly connected with the play. When I took the pitch first I
could hardly breathe, such was the heat and humidity, and it took me
some time to get my second wind.

Then there were the closing minutes of the game, by which time
Brazil were leading 4·1 and the Scottish players, resigned to defeat,
allowed their thoughts to stray to more personal considerations. In
the final minute, Zico, who had scored Brazil's equaliser direct from

Action from the same game. Steve Archibald and I in a tussle with Bryan Robson and Glenn Hoddle.

a free kick, suddenly found himself very popular with the opposition. But the five or six Scots marking him closely weren't so much interested in getting the ball from him as hoping to be closest to the star Brazilian when the final whistle sounded to claim his shirt in the after-match exchange.

The players who failed in this quest then had to dash elsewhere to settle for one of the lesser-known opponents.

I was more firmly established in the Scotland team by the time the 1986 World Cup finals came around, but this time bad luck, in the shape of illness, reduced my involvement and spoiled my enjoyment of the occasion.

After playing against Denmark in the opening Group E game in Mexico City — a match which I thought we were very unlucky to lose 1·0 — we moved to Queretaro to meet West Germany, but the night before the game I fell ill. It wasn't the dreaded Montezuma's Revenge: more like flu symptoms, but as far as I was concerned, just as effective in laying me low.

On the morning of the match, I felt slightly better and thought I would be OK for the game, but Alex Ferguson wisely insisted on a fitness test and I soon realised that I wouldn't last more than ten minutes.

Willie Miller gained his 50th cap in that game, but there wasn't much else for Scotland to celebrate when we were beaten 2-1 after Gordon Strachan had given us the lead.

This left us requiring a victory over Uruguay in the final game back in Mexico City to qualify for the second phase. It was one of the biggest disappointments of my career when the manager took me aside and told me he was leaving me out against Uruguay in favour of Dave Narey, who had taken my place against West Germany. Even Dave himself was surprised, fully expecting that I would be restored.

Naturally, I was bitterly disappointed and took the setback badly, going into a huff with the manager for the rest of our stay in Mexico, although looking back, I now realise that I wasn't being fair to Fergie, who was only doing what he thought best for the team.

Maybe he thought I hadn't fully recovered from my bout of flu, and I don't suppose the fact that he was my manager at both club and international levels made the decision any easier for him.

Happily, though, the manager and I had a long talk on our return to Scotland and that cleared the air, neither of us being the type to harbour a grudge for very long.

The 0-0 draw with Uruguay, of course, ended our qualifying hopes. On reflection, I don't think Scotland have so far ever had a better chance of qualifying for the second phase than we had in Mexico. Thinking about the Denmark game in particular, I feel there's a danger of us paying too much respect to teams we've heard a lot about in advance. Quite honestly, we should have beaten Denmark.

The trip to the 1986 World Cup finals, however, produced more happy memories than sad ones, particularly in the preparation period in the United States prior to moving on to Mexico.

After our altitude acclimatisation in Santa Fe, which was conducted in a relaxed atmosphere, we had a couple of friendlies in Los Angeles, and I remember in particular a shopping expedition we made in Beverley Hills, where some of the shops are so exclusive that you practically have to have an appointment to get in.

While Steve Archibald and I were walking along Rodeo Drive, where all these high-class shops are, I was hailed by Rikki Simpson,

The Aberdeen contingent return from the World Cup finals in Mexico. Alex Ferguson and I are not on speaking terms, but our differences were soon settled.

an Aberdeen publican who was in LA visiting his friend, pop star Rod Stewart.

Rod's a great Scotland fan and he wanted to throw a party at his Beverley Hills mansion for the Scotland squad. That, of course, was a non-starter as Alex Ferguson wouldn't hear of it so close to the start of the finals, so Rod had to settle for meeting some of the players over a cup of coffee.

After our surprise meeting with Rikki, Stevie and I went into one of the expensive shops selling designer clothes. Stevie quite fancied a shirt and while we were looking at it, Charlie Nicholas, Graeme Souness and Frank McAvennie came in and started buying some things.

This human pyramid, with me coming out on top, above England's Peter Withe and my Scottish team-mate Asa Hartford, is a reminder of Scotland's 1981 victory at Wembley — a feat we have not repeated since!

Encouraged by this, Stevie not only bought his shirt but a lot more besides. Eventually we left the shop, the others carrying several hundreds of pounds worth of purchases and me with a carrier bag and a brochure!

Alex Ferguson's commitment as Scotland manager ended with our return from Mexico and this brought me in contact with yet another international 'boss' in Andy Roxburgh. It also led to a minor hiccup in my international career, which I'll tell you about in the next chapter, which is devoted to my associations with and impressions of managers at club and international levels.

9

Please, Boss!

Although I've had only one senior club, you could say my experience of managers has been fairly wide-ranging: I've been associated with lots of managers at both club and national levels.

Two of these, Ally MacLeod and Alex Ferguson, I've known in both these roles, which while differing in many aspects are also similar in others. In man-management, for example, both jobs require the same qualities.

I may simply have been lucky, but I can honestly say that, widely as these managers differed from each other in temperament and personality, I've enjoyed excellent relations with each of them. There have been the occasions, of course, when we haven't seen eye to eye

I receive some special coaching from the Big Man himself, Jock Stein.

over some minor matter or other, but these have all been fleeting upsets ending with no hard feelings on either side.

The nearest approach to a serious rift in good relations, I suppose, was the occasion I referred to when I 'took the huff' with Alex Ferguson over being left out of the Scotland team for the Uruguay game in the World Cup finals in Mexico.

As I explained, I later realised that I was being unfair to the manager, wounded pride blinding me to his viewpoint. Fortunately, our temporary difference of opinion was very temporary.

Obviously, a player gets to know his club manager much more closely than he would a national team manager, and something else the reader should bear in mind is that my relationship with each of the various managers I mention has been basically different in that our association came at a different stage of my own career and stage of maturity.

For example, you wouldn't expect the relationship between a manager and a teenage ground-staff boy to be the same as that between him and an experienced, mature senior professional.

Allowing for that, I have found it fascinating over the years to observe the different ways in which the various bosses we have had at Pittodrie operated to achieve the common objective of getting the best out of their players.

Ally MacLeod, for instance, was the supreme 'wind-up' artist. As a ground-staff boy, I remember how he used to provoke certain players into greater effort by getting them annoyed. Goalkeeper Bobby Clark, in particular, seemed to take the bait every time.

It might be during a practice game with one team leading, say, 8-5, that Ally would suddenly announce 'the next goal is worth four'. The idea, of course, was to get the losing team back into contention quickly, but if it happened that Clarkie was in the side leading 8-5 and lost a goal to find themselves 8-9 down, the big keeper used to get real angry.

Generally, though, I think that Ally's methods, although they may have seemed a bit harebrained to us at the time, were effective. I know that if I get angry in matches or in training, it motivates me.

A bubbly character, with an infectious enthusiasm, Ally could be strict in matters of discipline. There was one occasion when he fined two reserve-team players for drinking cokes in an Aberdeen hotel after a game. I can vouch for this story because I was one of the players involved!

Dougie Brown, a player who joined the Dons at the same time as I did (and who, incidentally, is now in Australia where I met him when Scotland played in Melbourne in 1985), shared digs with me in the Woodend area of the city, and after this midweek reserve game — I think it was a Tuesday night — we were driving up Union Street on our way home when we realised that the manager's car was in front of us.

We knew he had seen us in his rearview mirror, recognising the car we were in, a Mini lent us by our landlady, and Dougie suggested that we slow down and let Ally's car get farther ahead of us. This was because we didn't want to be seen popping into a Queen's Road hotel for an after-match drink (honestly, it really WAS only cokes we had: although I was over 18, I hadn't by then progressed to the occasional beer, while Dougie was driving the car, so he was on soft drinks as well).

Anyway, thinking no-one was watching, we had our drink and thought nothing more of the incident. The following morning, however, we were playing table tennis when coach George Murray (another former clubmate I met in Australia) announced: 'McLeish and Brown, the boss wants you in his office.'

It must have been a guilty conscience, but I felt as if I was back at school being summoned to the headmaster's room to answer for some misdeed. I could feel myself flushing and the adrenalin was flowing.

'Did you go straight home last night?' was the manager's innocent-sounding first question. Like lambs to the slaughter, we said we had.

'You may think you're devious, but you'll find I'm an even more devious b . . . . . . ,' was Ally's reply and then he revealed that when we dropped back behind his car the previous night, he had gone right round the next roundabout, retracing his route along Queen's Road until he spotted our car in the hotel car park.

When I protested that we had only had a coke, he said: 'It'll be the dearest cokes you ever had. You're both fined a tenner.'

I believe that Ally still tells that story, although by now the fine he imposed is related as £300. I suppose that's what they mean by inflation!

At the time, though, I was worried by the incident and I asked George Murray, for whom I did some baby-sitting, if he thought it would count against me in the manager's eyes. I was mightily relieved when George reassured me that the fine was meant as a sharp lesson and the offence would soon be forgotten.

I was still in the reserves at the time Ally was Aberdeen's manager, so I didn't have any direct experience of how he handled the first-team players, but I was still able to appreciate what he did for the club as a whole.

His bubbling enthusiasm had the players, and everyone else at Pittodrie, believing in themselves once more, and with his tremendous flair for public relations, he had the club being talked about again as a potential force in Scottish football.

So it came as a big disappointment to us when Ally, after leading Aberdeen to a League Cup win in 1976, left Pittodrie to take up the Scotland manager's job, but fortunately he was succeeded by one of the living legends of Scottish football in Billy McNeill, who continued the revival of the club's fortunes started by Ally.

As I've mentioned before, Billy gave me my first first-team chance, but more importantly, I owe a lot to him for the help he gave me personally as a fellow centre half.

His commanding presence drew players to him and he liked an audience, so whenever he was speaking about some aspect of football there were always five or six players round him listening intently.

In day-to-day training, in which I saw most of him because I was still a reserve-team player for the most part, Billy was usually very matey and 'one of the boys' in his attitude, but there was never any doubt who was boss. I remember seeing him tear a player to shreds on one occasion, proving that he had the hardness needed for a successful manager.

On a few occasions I also experienced his wrath after a match for some mistake I had made, but almost invariably he would draw me aside the next day and explain his criticism in a constructive way.

It has been a long-standing complaint by Aberdeen players and managers that the national Press, based mostly in Glasgow, are prejudiced against any club which looks as if it might threaten the predominance of Rangers and Celtic, and it was, of all people, Billy McNeill who, for me, gave most substance to that theory. I remember him saying that he had never been aware of this West of Scotland media bias until he came to Aberdeen and experienced it from the other side of the fence, so to speak.

Alex Ferguson, of course, was the manager who had the biggest influence on me, partly because of the length of our association, and partly because he was there at the time that my football career was just coming to fruition.

In the early years of Fergie's managership at Pittodrie, he and the first-team players of that time were growing up together, although I think we players tended to forget to make allowances for the fact that the manager, too, was still learning his job, just as we were ours.

Some of the older players, for example, felt that the new manager harked back too often to the players he had had at St Mirren, citing them as paragons of this or that quality, as if he considered them better players than his present charges. But in due course Fergie himself realised that this was the wrong approach. Another lesson had been learned!

'Mercurial' was certainly one of the adjectives which could be applied to Fergie's personality. He could switch from high good humour to apparent fury, and back again in the space of a few minutes. I use the word 'apparent' because there was often a suspicion that the anger wasn't real, although it was convincing enough.

The problem was to decide when he was pretending to be angry and when he really *was* angry. It was a tricky business with dire consequences if you got it wrong.

I remember one occasion when Mark McGhee and I were getting a lift back from training in the boss's car, and on the way to Pittodrie we were passed by John Hewitt's car. John overtook us quite safely, but Mark, sensing an opportunity for a wind-up, said: 'Look at that, boss! There could have been an accident and think of the value of the players involved.'

'Aye, you're right. Just wait till we get back to the ground,' said the manager, and, sure enough, when he caught up with the 'offender' in the treatment room (an appropriate location you might think), he delivered a tongue-lashing which left poor John white-faced and shaken. If the manager hadn't winked at me before going into the treatment room, I would have been utterly convinced that his anger was real.

Whether Fergie's combination of bullying and jollying would have been as effective with older, more established players is open to argument, but it certainly worked with us as a young group growing up together. His record of success speaks for itself.

In his present position with Manchester United, Fergie probably has found himself working more with established players then he was at Pittodrie, but I'm prepared to bet that if they don't bow to his

Jock Stein's 'sparring partner', Celtic and Scotland masseur Jimmy Steel (centre) in more serious mood than usual as he watches an incident in an Aberdeen-Celtic game at Pittodrie. Also in the Celtic dugout are physiotherapist Brian Scott, manager David Hay and substitute Mark McGhee, while Aberdeen assistant manager Willie Garner is in the home dugout.

methods, he will have no hesitation in bringing in players who will conform. He has the ruthlessness of a man who must have success, no matter whose toes he has to stand on to achieve it. Big names don't mean anything to him.

When it came to the colourful phrase, Fergie showed originality and a vivid imagination. I used to think that he sat at home dreaming them up. They certainly got his message across.

The player being told 'I've seen more life in a dead slug' could hardly fail to get the point. Then there was the player who was being criticised for missing a chance because he had been tackled before he could get in his shot. 'I didn't think there was anyone near me' was his excuse, to which the boss replied: 'Where did you think you were — the b . . . . . Sahara desert?'

There was also a time when he accused me of having 'tunnel

vision' because I kept putting passes along the same route instead of switching them to different areas.

Extremely articulate, Fergie could deliver a brilliant team talk, but occasionally his tongue would run away with him and he would get some of the names mixed up. On one occasion, his attempt at the Dundee United pair Hegarty and Narey came out sounding like Negarty and Hairy. I never quite knew if that was a deliberate slip.

Nowhere was Alex Ferguson more effective as a speaker, though, than in persuading players to sign a new contract. Personally, I used to dread these contract negotiations because I knew that no matter how well I prepared my arguments beforehand, I would go in there and he would have me signed before I knew what had hit me. It would probably be the next day before you realised that you had re-signed, when you read it in the newspapers.

Fergie's first assistant at Pittodrie was Pat Stanton, whose personality in many ways was in sharp contrast to that of the manager, but they complemented each other magnificently. Pat was the calm, thoughtful character who frequently came along to mend relationships with a quiet word of exaplanation to the player whose feelings had been ruffled in a brush with the manager.

With Archie Knox, the relationship between manager and assistant was different. These two kept up a steady barrage of banter, to strike sparks off each other, but the understanding between them was phenomenal. Fergie found in Archie, I feel, a soul mate, someone who, like himself, lived and breathed football twenty-four hours a day, seven days a week. They would go anywhere to watch a football match, and it didn't matter too much what the standard of the teams was.

Another trait which Archie had in common with the manager was that he, too, had an excellent command of colourful language.

When Archie struck out on his own as manager of Dundee, Fergie took his time in choosing a successor before finally settling on Willie Garner, who had been doing well as player-manager of Alloa.

The move didn't work out as well as was hoped and Archie Knox's return to Pittodrie after the 1986 World Cup finals — this time as co-manager — saw Willie move on to positions with Highland League clubs Cove Rangers and then Keith.

Looking back, I suppose Willie was just a little too inexperienced at that time for the Pittodrie job. Coming as successor to Archie, he had no problems getting respect from the older players. Those of us who had played alongside him were all anxious for big Willie to succeed, but I think he should have been a bit firmer with the younger boys and exerted his authority more. On reflection, Willie himself would probably agree with that assessment.

The double departure of Alex Ferguson and Archie Knox for Manchester United in November, 1986 hit everyone at Pittodrie very hard but when, following a period of intense speculation, with dozens of household names mentioned as possible candidates, the appointment of Ian Porterfield came out of the blue, it was possibly just what the club needed at that stage.

The team hadn't started the 1986-87 season too well, going out to Celtic on penalties in the quarter-final of the Skol League Cup; losing to FC Sion in the first round of the European Cup-Winners' Cup; and suffering four defeats in our first seventeen Premier Division games.

The new manager, more familiar with the English soccer scene, came to us knowing little about the individual Aberdeen players except by reputation, but this, in fact, provided an extra stimulus, for most of us felt we had to prove ourselves to the new boss. Following his appointment, we ran up a series of fiteen league games without defeat and went out to Celtic in the third round of the Scottish Cup, but only after three games. Not too bad for a season of traumatic transition!

At the end of the day, though, I don't think we were good enough to win honours, but the manager quickly realised this and set about bringing in fresh blood with the signing of quality players like Peter Nicholas and, after that, Charlie Nicholas, while exploiting his knowledge of English football and his contacts south of the border to search for more personality players.

Ian Porterfield was very different in personality from Alex Ferguson, or, for that matter, from Billy McNeill and Ally MacLeod. They're all much more extrovert characters, but, like his predecessors, he's a keen and observant student of the game and has very definite views on how it should be played. From my own observations, I would say that his basic principle is that football should be kept as simple as possible, and when you consider that among the notable exponents of that philosophy are Liverpool, who can argue against it?

I was among the Aberdeen players who benefited from Ian Porterfield's arrival in that I felt the need to impress the new boss, and I think my game was given a fresh lift by that, which, in turn, added to my confidence.

With hindsight, though, I'd say Ian Porterfield's English background eventually proved a handicap, and possibly the major mistake he made was in not having as his No 2 someone who was well versed in the Scottish game. I say this with no disrespect to his assistant, Jimmy Mullen, who's a very likeable person.

Because neither the manager nor his assistant was familiar with Scottish teams and their players, they found themselves looking for guidance in these matters to the senior Aberdeen players, who really had enough on their plates concentrating on playing against the other teams without becoming involved in other areas.

There was also a danger of the younger Pittodrie players becoming resentful if the older ones were seen to be too much involved with the managerial team.

Ian Porterfield certainly didn't have much luck in his eighteen-month stay at Pittodrie. The job he had, following in the footsteps of Alex Ferguson, was difficult enough without having to contend with the severe problems which arose through no fault of his own.

In both the Skol League and the Scottish Cup, we came agonisingly close last season to achieving the kind of success he needed to win public acceptance, and if the outcome had been different, I feel sure he would have been able to overcome the adverse publicity to which he was subjected.

As you would gather, I like Ian Porterfield very much as a person, and I think in more favourable circumstances he could have been a success as Aberdeen's manager.

There's no doubt that the personal problems he experienced added greatly to the strain he was working under, and when I met him shortly after his resignation, he was a much more relaxed person. He could possibly have borne the pressure on himself, but when it began to affect his family too, it was that bit harder to bear.

With most other Scottish clubs, Aberdeen's record under Ian Porterfield would have been regarded as highly respectable, but the success the Dons enjoyed in the early '80s made it impossible for any manager to survive as a 'nearly' man. Only further triumphs will satisfy.

At the time of writing this, during the close season, I've still to experience what it is like working under the new Pittodrie management team of co-managers Alex Smith and Jocky Scott and assistant Drew Jarvie, but from my association with Alex and Jocky at the SFA coaching courses at Largs and with Drew as a former teammate, I see no reason why it shouldn't be a successful combination.

The idea of a management team as opposed to an individual manager is a comparatively recent development which seems to be growing in popularity as the most effective way of running a big football club in present day circumstances.

In the last resort, of course, there has to be one person who has the final say in such a set-up, and in our case it's Alex who carries this responsibility, but it's the corporate strength of the new backroom team, with these three very experienced and respected individuals — backed up, as always, by the invaluable Teddy Scott — each making a significant contribution in ideas and opinions, which probably holds the greatest promise.

I personally was delighted when I heard that Alex Smith was joining the Pittodrie staff before Ian Porterfield resigned because when we were at Largs, I found him very knowledgeable about the game, a sound tactician, and a top-class coach.

Following his appointment as co-manager, I heard some people wondering if he was 'too nice a guy' to be a good manager, but I can assure you he can be as tough and ruthless as anyone when it becomes necessary. I've seen him reduce seasoned professionals who had stepped out of line to quivering jellies on a couple of occasions.

Jocky was another one who impressed me at Largs with his confident manner and organisational skills, and has proved his managerial ability at Dundee.

As for Drew, I'm delighted to have such a great guy back at Pittodrie, and although I don't know what he's like on the coaching side, Jocky obviously thinks highly of him.

One of the early changes the new management team made to our routine last summer was to revert to our former practice, started in Ally MacLeod's day, of doing some of our pre-season training at Gordonstoun, the Morayshire boarding school whose high reputation in educational circles has been broadened into a more general fame by the attendance of several members of the Royal Family.

For the footballer accustomed to living in plush hotels when away from home, Gordonstoun is certainly quite a change — spartan living quarters with dormitory-type sleeping accommodation and canteen food — but the facilities for training are first class and the staff, from the ladies in the dining hall to George Welsh, who up to a couple of years ago was head of PE at the school, are tremendously friendly and helpful.

The worst thing about Gordonstoun, though, is the flies. At the time of year when we're there, they're horrendous, and in such numbers that it's well nigh impossible to ecape their attentions.

I remember on one of our early visits, Neil Simpson produced pyjamas as his night wear. This didn't quite fit in with our macho image of ourselves and the next day 'The Phantom' struck. Simmy's pyjamas were soon adorning the flagpole on the dormitory roof!

Needless to say, nobody has since dared to include such refinements when packing for that trip.

Training at Gordonstoun has alway been fairly intensive, with sessions morning, afternoon and evening. After that, it's a case of falling into bed in a heap, but after a spell there you're fully primed for the season ahead. When you come through the Gordonstoun experience unscathed, it gives you a real sense of achievement.

In an international context, the most impressive manager I have served under was, without doubt, Jock Stein.

I mentioned in an earlier chapter the consideration Jock showed in consoling me for a personal disappointment, but that, I must admit, was a side of his nature he didn't often reveal in public.

Although he enjoyed a good laugh as well as anyone, and entered into the spirit of things when his good friend Jimmy Steel (the Scotland squad masseur who doubles as court jester) was going through his vastly entertaining repertoire of impersonations, Jock was not the kind of manager any player dared to take liberties with.

He wore authority like a glove and anyone who, in his view, had stepped out of line, be he player, official, or Pressman, was quickly quashed, but he always treated his players as adults.

The combination of such a dominant personality and the seemingly physical indestructibility of a man who had survived a horrific motorway crash made it all the more difficult to credit his death from a heart attack at the end of a match which virtually booked Scotland a place in the World Cup finals in Mexico.

The trauma of that Tuesday evening at Ninian Park, Cardiff in September, 1985 was highlighted for me by the reaction of Alex Ferguson, who was Jock's assistant at the time.

When the match ended, we knew that Jock had been taken ill, but little more than that, and Fergie was anxious that we should stay on the pitch to acknowledge the cheers of the Scottish fans before going to the dressing room.

Most of us had showered and dressed when Fergie entered the dressing room and slumped into a chair near the door without uttering a word.

'Any news, boss?' I asked, and it was as if my voice had aroused him from a private reverie. He started, looked up and said simply: 'Jock's dead.'

I don't recall much about the rest of that night. I think the whole party returned to Scotland in a mental vacuum, such was the profound sense of shock and loss. The attendance at Jock's funeral is something I'll never forget — a moving tribute to the unique place Jock Stein had earned for himself in Scottish folklore.

When Alex Ferguson fulfilled his declared intention of giving up the Scotland managership after Mexico, there was a lot of speculation as to who would succeed him, but the appointment, when it came, of Andy Roxburgh really was a surprise to most, mainly because, although he was known and highly respected all over the football world in his capacity as SFA Director of Coaching, Andy, unlike all his predecessors as Scotland team manager, had had no experience of management at club level.

This was a bold and imaginative step by the SFA, but I feel that if anyone can prove the doubters wrong, Andy Roxburgh has a better chance than most. Like Alex Ferguson, he is extremely thorough in his preparation, and a great communicator of his ideas.

It was Jock Stein, I think, who once asked to be judged on whether he took Scotland to the World Cup finals — in fact, he was in charge for two successful qualifying campaigns — and I would think that Andy would be content to accept a similar judgement of his handling of the Scotland squad aiming to qualify for Italy in 1990.

At one point early in Andy's reign, I was beginning to think my international career was over. Injury forced me to withdraw from the squads for the European championship qualifying games against Bulgaria and Eire in September and October, 1986 with Dave Narey and Richard Gough respectively taking over the No 5 shirt, and the bush telegraph had it that the new manager was keen to adopt the English-style square formation for the back four.

It was a disappointment because I felt I still had something to contribute to the national team. But I consoled myself with the thought that with forty-odd caps behind me, I had had a good run, and the end of the road had to come sometime. In any case, the first thing, as it always had been, and always will be, was to maintain my form for my club.

At the same time, the doubt over my international future pro- bably acted as another little spur. It gave me the added incentive to demonstrate game by game for my club that I was still worthy of international consideration.

In the event, I was invited to attend the international get-together at Gleneagles at the end of January 1987 and re-entered the inter- national arena, by the back door if you like, as an over-age player and the captain of the Under-21 squad against Eire at Easter Road.

When Andy phoned me to discuss the idea, I said I would be delighted to skipper the colts' side, but that I hadn't abandoned my ambitions of playing for the full team. His reply was that he would have been disappointed if I had felt any other way, and he went on to explain that he planned that after the Under-21 game I should join the senior squad, who were playing Eire at Hampden the following night.

The same system was to have operated for the away games against Belgium in April, but this time I was called up from the Under-21 to the full squad and played against Belgium in Brussels. It wasn't the most auspicious occasion to return to the side: we played a zonal defence and Belgium, with a team tailor-made to exploit this particular defensive system, hit us on the break to win 4-1.

For the less technically-minded, zonal defence is an alternative system to the one most commonly employed in British football which has a sweeper operating behind a stopper centre half. As its name suggests, zonal defence has defenders operating in their own particular areas of the pitch, another defender taking over respon- sibility when an attacking run moves from one zone to another. Doing without an out-and-out sweeper, it's a more economical sys- tem with all the defenders covering for each other, but it requires some practice to employ successfully and we hadn't had enough time to go into it thoroughly enough before the Belgian game.

After being called in to captain the Scotland B team in a 1-1 draw with France at Pittodrie at the end of April, I played in both Rous Cup matches against England and Brazil, but the 1987-88 season started with another disappointment when injury put me out of the squad for the Hampden friendly against Hungary in September.

I was back in the Scotland squad when the Belgians were the visitors in October, but I didn't expect a place in the team as Richard Gough and Willie Miller had teamed up in central defence against Hungary and the manager wanted to give them another run together. But both Richard and Willie had to withdraw with injuries and their bad luck was good luck for me because I was called on to form a new central defensive partnership with Gary Gillespie and Scotland went on to beat Belgium 2-0.

Gary and I were still together in the next European game when we beat Bulgaria 1-0 in Sofia in November, and that made me feel as if I had re-established myself in the team — a feeling which was confirmed the following month when I was given the team captaincy against Luxembourg to mark my 50th cap.

The recall against Belgium was a lucky break for me, but before being selected I began to think Dame Fortune really had it in for me.

Travelling south to join the Scotland squad on the Sunday in a car borrowed from a friend, I had my first hint of trouble ahead when the car engine began to give out strange noises. Finally, I gave up the unequal contest a couple of miles south of Laurencekirk and pulled into the side of the road.

My first attempt to seek assistance at a nearby farmhouse was speedily abandoned when I spotted a Doberman snoozing in the porch, and after failing to get an answer at the next couple of houses, I decided to try to hitch a lift back to Laurencekirk.

Dressed casually and sporting one of my frequent eye wounds which scarcely improved my appearance, I wasn't exactly the ideal candidate for a successful hitch-hiker, but eventually I was recognised and picked up by a young chap travelling north with his girl friend.

He took me to Laurencekirk where I went into a pub in search of a phone. The phone there was out of order, but my face again came to the rescue as some of the lads in the bar recognised me and one of them took me to his home to use the phone. I called my father-in-law Danny Taylor in Aberdeen and he drove down, towed my friend's car back to a garage in Laurencekirk, and then transported me back to Stonehaven to catch a train to Glasgow.

All in all, it was a roundabout way to travel from Aberdeen to Glasgow, and I was over four hours late for the official rendezvous time. I was expecting to be in hot water, but Andy Roxburgh and the other members of his staff just laughed when they heard my story.

10

The Triangle

Willie Miller? What can I say about my 'alter ego' that hasn't been said before — and won't sound as if I'm sucking up to the team skipper?

Seriously, though, I have a great admiration for Willie on and off the pitch, and I'm even prepared to put up with being kept awake by his snoring when we're sharing a hotel room while away with either Aberdeen or Scotland. I hasten to add that it's not something he often inflicts on me, and I mention it only because I can't think of anything else about him to find fault with.

The Triangle — Jim Leighton, Willie Miller and myself with Ian Porterfield.

On reflection, I suppose, the happy knack which Willie has of being able to take a nap anytime and anywhere — when he isn't counting his money, that is — is just another indication of the relaxed kind of person he is off the field.

I don't quite know why, but Willie and I get on as well together off the field as we do on it. It's not that we're exactly alike in make-up — Willie's the private, self-contained type, while I'm probably more of an extrovert. And it isn't that we're so different we complement each other. Our relationship is as difficult to describe as it is to analyse, but it's a solid friendship, based on mutual respect and liking.

As in most friendships, we do have the occasional falling-out, but they have almost always been on the field in the heat of battle and never continued after the game is over.

I remember one occasion, I think it was a game against Dundee United, when we almost came to blows. But the minute we squared up we both realised how ridiculous the situation was and burst out laughing. We were expecting our behaviour would bring a reprimand from Alex Ferguson after the game, so it was a pleasant surprise when he commended us instead. He interpreted our outburst as a measure of how deeply involved we were in the game.

Regular followers of the Dons will have noticed the ritual Willie and I go through during the pre-match warm-up sessions when we work as a pair, passing the ball back and fore and giving each other heading practice, etc.

I can't quite remember how it started, but this is just something which has developed over the years and I think it has become almost a superstition for both of us and we would feel it strange if we departed from the usual formula. It has a practical purpose too. The inter-passing part of the exercise helps us to assess the hardness and bumpiness or otherwise of the pitch, while the heading sharpens up our reactions and timing just before the game.

On the occasions that Willie isn't playing I don't seem to feel the same compulsion to follow the routine, although I sometimes do a midfield routine with whoever is deputising for him.

I'm frequently asked how the great understanding on the pitch between Willie and myself developed and I find this difficult to answer. It just seemed to happen that the chemistry was right, and I'm happy that it did because I know that playing alongside Willie Miller has helped my game tremendously over the years at both club and international levels. Hopefully, I've been able to do something for his game, in which I would say one of the most important elements is his superb consistency.

Of course, playing together so often has contributed a lot to our understanding — a recent check revealed that of my 550-odd first-team appearances for Aberdeen, more than 450 of them have been with Willie alongside me in central defence, and we've performed similarly in double harness for Scotland about forty times.

There have been many other examples of successful partnerships such as this in the history of football, but most of them have been goal-scoring combinations between two strikers.

It has something to do with awareness, almost a sixth sense, which tells us where the other one is at any particular point in a game. Sometimes we add a brief, shouted word or two, but usually even that isn't necessary.

There was one occasion, though, when our telepathic understanding didn't work.

Willie has a terrible memory for names and it's not unusual for him to consult me before he goes to toss the coin to refresh his memory of the opposing captain's name. On this occasion, we were playing a certain Glasgow club, and when Willie came up to me, I anticipated his usual question and said before he could speak: 'It's Danny McGrain'. 'I know that, you idiot! That's no' what I was going to ask you,' he replied indignantly.

Whatever goes to produce our partnership, I'm convinced that when we're playing together, our joint contribution to the team effort is greater than the sum of our individual abilities, and I don't think I'm being unduly immodest when I say that if we're both in top form, we're capable of handling any attacking partnership you can name.

As our critics are quick to point out, neither Willie nor myself is the fastest thing on two feet, but there are ways and means of compensating for anything we lack in pace. Positioning; when to tackle and when not to; the timing of the tackle itself; and knowledge of the game acquired and sharpened by years of experience are all factors in effectively combating the superior speed of an opponent. We have proved that, I think, against some really top-class strikers such as Karl Heinz Rumenigge, Ian Rush, Mark Hughes etc.

On the subject of pace, I remember one occasion when moving too fast cost Willie half a steak. It was while we were dining during one of our overnight stays in the Excelsior at Glasgow Airport.

Willie was doing full justice to a fillet steak when he was paged to answer a phone call from his wife Claire. Not wanting to keep the 'boss' waiting, he dashed off at a greater pace than we had seen from him all week in training, leaving his unfinished steak on the plate.

When he returned a few minutes later, though, his plate was empty. Questioning the other lads at the table brought a succession of denials, but Gordon Strachan's protestations of innocence were less than convincing considering his cheeks were bulging as he tried to swallow half a fillet steak!

For all his quiet reserve, Willie can hold his own in the matter of practical jokes. There was the time that Alex Ferguson was aroused in the early hours of Sunday morning by a phone call and was treated to a rendition by the 'Mike Sammes Singers', the call coming from a Saturday night party some of us were having in Willie's house.

It was more than coincidence that Fergie decided that training on Monday should feature the dreaded 'Seaton Run' — the Aberdeen equivalent of Jock Wallace's commando course on Gullane sands, a rigorous stamina-building (or sapping) chase over rough, hilly terrain surrounding Seaton Park — and that the Mike Sammes Singers should be in the forefront of the running squad.

The manager's retaliation for the interruption of his sleep was marred only by the fact that Mike Sammes himself — our gallant captain — missed training that morning for some reason or other. For Willie, the Seaton Run held as much attraction as a cold bath at the North Pole.

Coolness under pressure is one of the hallmarks of Willie Miller's play, but I can recall one occasion when he 'lost his cool', although it wasn't on the football field.

When we were selected for the international squad for the 1982 World Cup finals in Spain, Willie, Steve Archibald and myself decided to take our wives and families and stay on for a holiday after the finals.

The idea was to house the three families, plus a couple of baby-sitters, in adjoining apartments in Marbella, but our bookings, as they have a way of doing, ran into problems and we found our accommodation scattered all over the place.

Trying to explain our difficulty to the concierge, Willie found that this gentleman's English was apparently no better than Willie's Spanish — and that's negligible!

Listening to the exchange, Steve and I were splitting our sides, both suspecting that the concierge's ignorance of the English language — apart from two words 'No posseeble' — was no more than a convenient screen against protesting Scots.

Willie must have reached the same conclusion for he became increasingly heated. Just when he seemed ready to make his point more forcibly, Steve and I quickly intervened before any physical damage could be done and managed to calm down the concierge, who by this time was all for phoning for police assistance.

Eventually, we had to get back on to our travel agent to sort out the accommodation problem.

If the names Miller and McLeish are almost invariably linked together, they're usually accompanied in the same breath by a third — Leighton. 'The Triangle', the late Jock Stein used to call us: a team within a team, now sadly broken up at club level but hopefully continuing in the international squad.

Like the longer-standing partnership between Willie and myself, the more recent defensive trio didn't just suddenly happen: it developed gradually with all three of us working on its development, analysing our mistakes in post-match discussions, and encouraging each other during games.

I first came across Jim Leighton when we were schoolboys. He attended a school in Johnstone, St Cuthbert's I think it was, when I was at Barrhead High School and we played against each other frequently. We were both with Glasgow United, although Jim was in a different team, being a year ahead of me at school, and Bobby Calder brought us north to Aberdeen for summer training at the same time. But Jim had a spell in junior football with Dalry Thistle and became a full-timer at Pittodrie a couple of years after me.

You would scarcely credit it now, but a scout once told Jim: 'You're a great goalie, son, but you're too wee'.

In those days, he was a bit small for a keeper, but, like myself, he stretched in his late teens. I used to kid him that his father must have hung him from the crossbar with weights on his feet, but I wouldn't have been surprised if Jim, with his dedication to improving his game, had inflicted this torture on himself.

Jim shared my interest in table tennis and I remember both of us playing in the Renfrewshire schools junior championships. I don't let him forget that he was knocked out in the first round, while I went on to the final.

Starting with great natural talent, Jim has developed into the

Trying hard to be a Willie Miller look-alike I make an acceptance speech after receiv-
ing the Aberdeen Sports Council's Personality of the Year award on behalf of Willie in
November, 1987. Grampian director of education James Michie looks a bit puzzled.
'Is Willie Miller really that tall?' he could be asking himself.

world-class goalkeeper that he is by working extremely hard at his
job. I think he learned good habits early in his Pittodrie career as
understudy to Bobby Clark, for Clarkie was also a hard worker. Jim,
in his turn, gave a lot of help to the young goalkeepers on the Aberdeen staff.

When you see the Scotland squad goalkeepers doing their specialist training under coach Alan Hodgkinson, you realise that they
train as hard, if not harder, than we outfield players do.

Jim makes some spectacular, and sometimes almost impossible
saves, but it's in the small things, things that the spectator may not
notice or appreciate, that his real worth lies.

Jim's a great student of the game, and he'll look at the opposition's team list before a game and pick out any potential danger men
who have to be specially watched, say, in the air at corners and other
set-piece situations. Uusually at flag kicks, I take up position at the
rear of the six-yard box, ready to attack the ball when it comes over,
but if there's any opponent Jim thinks is particularly good in the air,
then I stick with him.

This is arranged before we go out on the field and Jim also has his
'wall' organised, who's to be at the posts for corners, etc. Big Jim is
definitely the 'boss' as far as the goalmouth is concerned. What he
says goes.

His thoroughness extends to his own pre-match preparation and
he's out on the pitch long before the rest of the team for his warm-up,
with one of the substitutes providing a variety of crosses and shots
for him.

The amount of thought Jim puts into the game has helped build
up his understanding with Willie and myself. One small illustration of
this understanding is the question of when a goalkeeper should
leave his line to challenge an attacker.

You often see instances in matches of goals coming from a striker making a breakthrough. He's being chased by a defender, who
might have a chance of getting in a tackle or putting him off in some
way, but the goalkeeper coming out makes up the striker's mind for
him and he has a go from longer range.

Jim tended to stay in his goal because his understanding with us
was such that he was able to assess accurately what chance the
chasing defender had of making a challenge and he would come out
only when he knew that it was the only hope left.

It is for these little tricks of the trade which only long experience
playing together can bring that we will miss Jim Leighton at
Pittodrie.

11

The Pittodrie Gang

Before Willie Miller became my regular room-mate, I used to share with John McMaster, who must have been one of the most popular players ever on the Pittodrie staff. Johnny seemed to get on well with everyone. He was so likeable and easy-going that he was often the target of other players' humour, but he took all that in good part.

One of our favourite recreations was inventing new nicknames for him, with Stuart Kennedy, who was the club's ace winder-up, leaving us all behind in that respect.

Willie Miller, Peter Nicholas and John Hewitt join me in welcoming Charlie Nicholas to Pittodrie.

Charlie and I join forces to open a nightclub for the disabled. This was the day after we had been put out of the Scottish Cup by Dundee United but we still managed a half-smile.

One time when the club took us on an end-of-season holiday in Majorca, we were all on the beach when Johnny, after a great deal of coaxing, finally persuaded me to share a pedalo with him. Johnny was wearing a colourful tee shirt, one of a number he had, and when we returned to the beach after being fairly far offshore, the rest of the lads claimed that they had been able to identify us among dozens of similar craft by Johnny's tee shirt alone.

While we had been away, however, Stuart had come up with a new nickname and for the next few days my room-mate became Johnny 'Cousteau'. Johnny's only response was to grumble: 'It was never going to be *Alex* Cousteau, was it?'

While on the subject of nicknames, one of my earliest at Pittodrie was 'John Boy', after one of the main characters in the popular tele-vison seres *The Waltons.* I think it was Davie Robb who thought it up, probably because of my red hair and freckly face. I spoke earlier about how Davie Robb set me at ease with a humorous remark

Happy families! Aberdeen players gather with their wives and children giving manager Alex Ferguson a problem in picking his 'youth' team.

before my competitive first-team debut, but Davie's sense of humour wasn't always so kindly. He was a master of heavy sarcasm, and I remember one of our overnight stays in Glasgow when the tea he was served with wasn't hot enough for his taste. 'Excuse me, love,' he said to the waitress, 'Do you think you could bring me another cup of COLD tea?'

Speaking of room partners reminds me of a story from a trip to Bulgaria for a European tie.

Gordon Strachan was sharing with Willie Garner — a case of Little and Large, you might say — and wee Gordon woke up in the middle of the night to see Willie affectionately clapping his Adidas travelling bag at the side of his bed and muttering 'Good dog, good dog.'

'Are you are all right, big man?' asked Gordon, but when Willie, obviously startled by the voice, glowered at his room-mate, Gordon realised that he had been talking in his sleep and decided to keep the right side of him by offering to 'take his bag for a walk.'

D

You can see why Dave Robb nicknamed me 'John Boy' after the *Waltons* character.

Wee Gordon was always quick with the repartee. Once when someone, rather tactlessly, asked him why the jacket he was wearing was liberally adorned with what obviously were soup stains, he replied: 'It's my dinner jacket.'

I've already identified Stuart Kennedy as winder-up-in-chief — a role which I took over when Stuart tragically had to give up football due to injury — and he was rarely at a loss for a get-out if the joke threatened to be at his expense.

The classic case of Stuart having the last word, I think, was the time Alex Ferguson was criticising the full back's crossing of the ball, describing his efforts as 'pathetic'.

Stuart protested that he had been working hard on this part of his game, returning to the ground in the afternoons for extra practice, and then he appealed to Archie Knox for confirmation.

'Aye, there's no doubt your crossing has improved,' Archie admitted.

'Oh, you mean improved to pathetic,' asked Stuart, and even Alex Ferguson had no answer to that.

Doug Rougvie, who became such a favourite with the Dons' fans before he moved to England, was just as much a 'character' in the dressing room as he was on the pitch.

The big Fifer, in the way of many who hail from that part of the country, prefaced all his remarks with 'Hey, sir', only it came out sounding more like 'Hessir!'

Doug was one of those people who seem to get themselves into hot water without even trying and then can't understand what they've done wrong.

During one close season, Alex Ferguson was horrified to read an article in Saturday's 'Green Final' featuring big Doug with a motor cyclist's helmet under his arm. The story revealed that Doug had bought a motor cycle and was considering going to the Isle of Man for the TT races. Whether to compete or watch, I'm not sure, but he was sharply talked out of that idea when the manager got hold of him.

'Get rid of that motor bike, or we'll be getting rid of you,' was the manager's reported ultimatum.

From motor bikes to push bikes, and still Doug Rougvie was in trouble. Just before a cup final, Doug, who had switched from motor to pedal power, was knocked off his bike in Mounthooly, but managed to conceal the accident, and his injuries, from the manager for three or four days before retribution eventually caught up with him.

Doug's outsize frame was useful on the football pitch, but it could have its disadvantages in everyday life. For example, when he jammed himself into a canoe during a pre-season stay at Gordonstoun, he came close to drowning before some of the other lads came to his rescue after the flimsy craft had turned over. He lost several layers of the skin on his hips before they prised him free of the canoe.

Doug became known as Sheriff Rougvie after one escapade during our Majorca holiday. At that time he was reading a lot of Westerns, and when the opportunity of doing some horse-riding in Majorca arose, he seized it as a chance to live out his cowboy fantasies.

Once the problem of finding a horse tall enough to take him without his feet trailing on the ground had been solved, Doug greeted his new-found friend with an affectionate slap on the head which must have rattled the poor horse's brains.

The patient nag gave him the benefit of the doubt, though, probably taking account of Doug being a Fifer, and allowed him to get on but when he continued to use these playful slaps as a means of urging his mount forward, the horse decided enough was enough and tried to bite Doug's hand every time it came within reach.

To most outsiders, Bobby Clark would seem the perfect gentleman — and so he was most of the time. But he could be on a short fuse at times, and when roused he wasn't someone to tangle with lightly because of his size and physical development which earned him the nickname of Clark Kent: he had only to take off his shirt and he became Superman.

I remember Clarkie once chasing Stuart Kennedy all round the Pittodrie car park after Stuart had made some remark. Stuart's speed of foot kept him clear of danger, but he was finally cornered in the dressing room, fearing the worst. But Clarkie had cooled down by this time and instead of tearing into Stuart as expected, he actually apologised to him for whatever he had done to prompt Stuart's remark.

Big Bobby used to take some stick from the other players about his heavy involvement in football coaching, but he could hold his own in these verbal skirmishes.

Once when the subject of nuclear warfare was being dicussed — you would be surprised how highbrow the Pittodrie dressing-room talk gets sometimes — Bobby said it would be a good idea to have a nuclear shelter built underneath his house, whereupon someone suggested that he should buy training cones so that he could hold coaching sessions for his wife Betty and the kids while they were in the shelter.

Quick as a flash, Bobby came back with: 'Aye, and I'll have to buy a gun as well. In the event of nuclear war, I would have to shoot any of you lot who came near the shelter.'

Ian Scanlon was another of the great characters we had at Pittodrie. He was a fine ball-player on his game, but he had great difficulty in making up his own mind about anything. Before a game he would go round the dressing room asking various team-mates what kind of boots they intended to wear.

With each reply, he would agree with that player's choice, but then change his mind if the next person he asked happened to give a different reply.

Some of the Pittodrie Gang — Stuart Kennedy, Gordon Strachan and myself sit out a
match at Pittodrie.

A highly-strung personality, Scan was easily upset before a game
and Gordon Strachan took advantage of this just after Scan had left
Aberdeen for St Mirren in part exchange for Peter Weir.

When we played Saints for the first time after the move, wee Gordon found himself beside Scan as the teams lined up for the kick-off.
As Gordon shook hands with his former clubmate, he slipped him a
folded piece of paper which Scan opened to find a demand for pay-
ment of a small account which he had forgotten to settle before leaving Aberdeen. The game was well on before Scan recovered his
composure.

I remember an occasion during his Pittodrie days when Ian, who
was unfailingly polite to everyone, took time off from a game to cor-
rect a spectator. He was wearing the No 11 shirt as usual and this fan
kept shouting: 'Scanlon get up your wing' until finally Ian stopped
and shouted back: 'I'm no' playin' on the wing today. The manager
says I've to play in midfield.'

In more recent times, another member of the 'St Mirren Connection' who livened up the Aberdeen dressing room for a period before

he, like Stuart Kennedy, had his top-class soccer career curtailed by injury, was Frank McDougall.

I regard Frank as the best natural finisher I've ever seen, scoring some phenomenal goals — four against Celtic in a league game at Pittodrie and hat-tricks against Rangers and Hearts to mention just some of his scoring achievements.

After his four-goal feat against Celtic, he modestly responded to our congratulations with: 'Don't call me Frank. Just call me King!'

A talented singer, especially when he moved up to falsetto rendering of the songs popularised by some of the coloured singing groups. Frank frequently told stories against himself.

One of these related to his time at St Mirren. After becoming a home-owner for the first time, he admitted to a team-mate that he had a worry. There were 'other people' living in his house and he didn't know what to do about it. Apparently he hadn't realised that he had bought only a part of the house, not the whole building.

In case you think that all my stories are about former Pittodrie players, I'll tell you one about Neil Simpson. No, this particular story has nothing to do with Simmy's prodigious appetite, about which a number of legends have grown.

We were puzzling over one of those trick questions which go the rounds: Which three footballers have surnames which are also names of countries?

We got Ally or Alan Brazil and Joe Jordan easily enough, but were stumped for a third one until Simmy, in a flash of inspiration, came up with 'Jock LiechtenSTEIN'. Quite an ingenious answer, I thought!

No selection of characters in the Pittodrie gang would be complete without mention of Teddy Scott.

Harold Edward Scott — 'Teddy' to everyone who is anyone in Scottish football except when some of us at Pittodrie call him 'Harry' as a joke — is probably the most important member of the Pittodrie staff.

If Teddy ever left Aberdeen FC, they would have to appoint three or four people to take his place, such is the volume and variety of the work he undertakes. But his greatest importance, I feel, lies in the role he plays in developing the talents of young players.

My dad's advice when I left home to join Aberdeen was: 'Always pay attention to your coaches, even if you don't always agree with what they're saying.'

Teddy is the first person a youngster has dealings with on coming

Dundee United striker Paul Sturrock, one of the victims of Teddy Scott's sense of humour in Santa Fe, attempts to get past Jim Bett and myself.

to Pittodrie, and, as such, he has a tremendous influence on new-comers at the most formative stage of their professional careers. The good habits instilled in players at that age remain with them.

It's a measure of the close personal interest Teddy takes in every one of his charges that when players who have subsequently left Pittodrie for other clubs pay return visits, he's invariably the first person they ask for.

Totally respected by young and elder players alike at Pittodrie, Teddy is another of those rare characters who join in dressing-room banter without sacrificing any of their authority.

The high regard in which Teddy is held isn't confined to the Aberdeen club. He is known and equally respected at football clubs the length and breadth of Scotland, including outposts such as the Western Isles and Shetland, where he has done valuable pioneer work by taking teams to play there.

If they ever had a testimonial match for Teddy, they would have to hire Hampden!

Long experience with young players has given Teddy a sixth sense for detecting any player 'swinging the lead'. On the Seaton Run, in particular, it's almost as if he is able to disguise himself as a tree and merge into the background. Whenever anyone is tempted to cheat a little by walking for a spell or taking a shortcut, you can bet Teddy will turn up at the right spot to put him back on the right track.

Never one to mince his words, Teddy can always be relied on to give an honest and frank assessment of a player's performance, but any criticism he may have is always tempered by an innate kindliness and concern for the player he's criticising.

I remember one occasion early in Gordon Strachan's Pittodrie career. It was before the wee man had fully established himself as a first-team regular, and he was having a spell in the reserves to find his form.

But thinking that he was ready for a first-team place, Gordon was waiting anxiously for the squads to be announced on the Friday when Teddy came into the dressing room, put an arm round Gordon's shoulders and said: 'You can be my captain at Rothienorman tomorrow'. It was his way of softening the blow for wee Gordon, who, as ever, kept the joke going by putting on a display of hysterical horror at the prospect.

Teddy's impish sense of humour showed again when he was on the Scotland staff for the World Cup finals in Mexico. During the Santa Fe preparations, he often helped Jimmy Steel with the massage sessions and once, when he was working on Eamonn Bannon, he casually remarked: 'Aye, you used to be danger man as far as Aberdeen were concerned.'

Then it was the turn of Eamonn's Dundee United clubmates Paul Sturrock and Richard Gough. When he said to Richard: 'I never saw anyone take you to the cleaners as John Hewitt did in the Skol Cup semi-final', all poor Richard could do was thank Teddy for that confidence-booster for the coming World Cup games.

Then there was the time we almost drowned Archie Knox.

It was during a mid-season training break in Spain when in a bout of high spirits the players tossed Archie into the swimming pool. We were commenting on how good he was at pretending to be a non-swimmer when we suddenly realised that he wasn't pretending, and in fact he couldn't swim, so a few of us dived in and pulled him out.

For once, Archie didn't have the last word — he could only splutter!

Mark McGhee, myself, Stuart Kennedy and John McMaster await a departure from Aberdeen Airport.

Many of the most amusing anecdotes to circulate among the Aberdeen players spring from the players' periodic contacts with the various Supporters' Club branches.

Two of these stories show how something a supporter might say in an unguarded moment could be quite hurtful to a player unless he had a strong sense of humour, as, I'm glad to say, most of my Pittodrie clubmates have.

There was the occasion, for instance, when Stewart McKimmie went to receive a Player of the Year award at one of the Supporters' Club branches. The chairman, in the course of his presentation speech, said: 'The winner of the award this season is Stewart McKimmie — personally, I voted for Alex McLeish . . .'

It was my turn to be the victim on another of these ocassions when an elderly woman supporter approached me and said: 'Ye ken this, Alex. I remember when ye were jist a young loon, I saw you playing for the reserves . . .' At this point I was fully expecting her to go on to say that even then she recognised my potential, so it came as something of a shock when she continued: 'And the thing that struck

E

me was that you had an awfa spotty face.' To add to my embarrassment, she then gave my cheeks a rub and added: 'My, it's like a baby's bum noo.'

Aberdeen supporters are often criticised for being a bit laid back at Pittodrie, and it's certainly true that the fans who travel with us seem to be more vocal in their support at away games, but it's small price to pay for the kind of supporters we have. When you meet in a one-to-one situation, such as Supporters' Club 'dos', they're very friendly.

I think Aberdeen is just that kind of city, and having only one Premier club to claim the support of its citizens makes it easier for a footballer to have a relatively normal life.

Shopping in Union Street can be done with little more than a nod or smile of recognition here and there and the odd comment on the team's current form. There's none of the pestering by the public that Rangers or Celtic players get in Glasgow.

Dons' supporters, of course, aren't to be found only in the Granite City itself. In fact, some of those who live furthest away from Aberdeen are among the most enthusiastic, particularly those in the Highlands and Islands.

On a recent visit to supporters on one of the Islands, I was given an insight into the different lifestyle they enjoy there. After being given a guided tour by car and shown all the tourist attractions, including a distillery, we reached the main street. There were perhaps three or, at the most, four cars coming up the street towards us when my guide remarked, in all seriousness: 'Och, I forgot it was the rush hour.'

12

The Scottish Game

Football in Scotland today has, and always has had, I suppose, its detractors, and it would be foolish to pretend that everything in our national game is entirely as it should be.

On the whole, I think the eighties can be rated a fairly healthy decade for Scottish football, domestically and internationally, considering the obstacles it has had to surmount — increasing competition from the so-called minority sports, and the hooligan element among spectators to mention just a couple.

As far as the Premier Division is concerned — and inevitably it is on the health of this elite group that the state of our domestic game is judged — a steady rise in attendances in each of the past few seasons would seem to indicate that the administrators are on the right track.

There have been other contributory factors, but a major cause, in my view, for this upsurge in public interest has been a see-sawing in the East-West power struggle.

In the first half of the decade, Aberdeen, and, to a lesser extent, Dundee United laid down a successful challenge to the domination of the Old Firm, who reacted to this breaking of their stranglehold on the major domestic trophies by launching into the big-money transfer market in an unprecedented manner.

This, in effect, returned the challenge to the East coast clubs, and although Aberdeen, Dundee United, and the two Edinburgh clubs may not be in the same league as Rangers in particular in financial resources, it is necessary nevertheless that the gauntlet thrown down by the Old Firm pair is taken up.

Hearts have shown in their revival of the last couple of seasons that they can mount a realistic challenge, while Hibs have also responded positively and hopefully can once more be a force to be reckoned with. The two Edinburgh clubs have energetic, go-ahead chairmen in Wallace Mercer and David Duff, and both appear determined to restore former glory to their respective clubs.

Most big football clubs experience fluctuations in which their levels of achievement move towards a peak and then dip, but it is essential for a club like Aberdeen that we are always challenging Celtic and Rangers for the domestic honours. Winning a trophy every few years is not enough for a club which has tasted the success that the Dons have in recent years, and the Pittodrie club cannot afford to let an appreciable gap develop between their standard and that of the Old Firm pair, because, once established, it would be difficult to bridge.

It isn't only in domestic competition that we've got to set our sights high. European football has become increasingly an area in which Scotland's top clubs are looking for success with reasonable hope of fulfilling their aims.

Thanks to the performances of Aberdeen, Dundee United, Rangers and Celtic on this stage, Scotland since 1984 has enjoyed the luxury of three qualifying places in the UEFA Cup draw, and this distinction, carrying with it prestige and the esteem of Continental nations, is something we've got to maintain.

Rangers' recent policy of spending prodigious sums of money to take big-name players to Ibrox may not have been fully reflected in results, but, apart from prompting rival clubs to cast a similarly wide net in the transfer market, it has had a valuable side-effect in getting Scottish football talked about not only in England, but across the Channel too.

I think that even in its amended format for promotion and relegation the Premier Division will still subdivide naturally each season into two competitions, with the same five, or perhaps six, clubs as live contenders for the championship title and the remaining clubs having avoiding relegation as their primary target.

While this seems almost inevitable for a number of reasons, I don't think it's necessarily a bad thing, as long as there are at least four or five clubs each capable of winning the title, and that the other clubs, while not having title-winning potential, are each competent enough to have days when they can take points off the championship contenders.

One of the drawbacks of a two-tier Premier Division and the cut-throat competition it produces, of course, is that it tends to make most teams concentrate on not losing games instead of winning them. I think it would be fair to say that Celtic are the only team who unfailingly place more emphasis on scoring goals than on preventing the opposition scoring. Having said that, I think a tightening up

Alan Ferguson is obviously not very happy with something I've done.

at the back was a significant factor in Celtic winning the Premier title last season. The result was that they won a fair number of games by a 1-0 margin, and it was also noticeable that their 'goals for' tally was lower than usual.

We at Pittodrie are going out to win each game just as much as our Parkhead rivals, but our style is slightly different. Over the years the Dons have been most effective when they can 'suck in' the opposition and hit them on the break. This is fine when the opposing team are willing to attack us, but when, as so often happens, a team comes to Pittodrie and plays five players at the back and only one up front, it can become most frustrating for the Aberdeen players and their supporters alike.

It is then that the fans have to show understanding of the team's problems and exercise the same kind of patience which, hopefully, the players are employing on the pitch. It's not easy, I admit, but it's a discipline we all have to accept.

It's a common complaint that we in Scotland play too many club matches, and I would agree that after a couple of seasons playing 44 Premier Division fixtures, it's something of a relief to get back to the 36-game league programme. But we still play each of the other Premier Division teams at least four times a season, and I feel that the familiarity with the opposition which this brings tends to stifle individual talent a bit.

An overabundance of fixtures is not the only way we Scots make it hard for ourselves. There is also the type of football we play — a hundred mile-an-hour stuff which takes its toll physically. Little wonder most players are more than a little jaded by the end of the season!

The typically British style of football, when methodically harnessed, can be a potent weapon against Continental opposition in the European competitions, but the Latin-type football certainly leaves more scope for developing ball skill.

Climatic conditions influence to some extent the kind of football favoured in a particular country, but the style of play found in the warmer countries has a lot going for it. Because the action in the Latin countries is more of the stop-go variety with the players making the ball do more of the work instead of their legs, ball control and accuracy in the long pass are more carefully studied and developed by practice.

It's claimed that British spectators wouldn't respond to a total diet of that slow build-up of attacks, and I suppose they would need some re-educating to appreciate it. The closest approach to it found in Britain is the build-up used by Liverpool — and their supporters don't seem to be complaining!

Between the number of games we play and the way we play them, Scottish football is a real pressure cooker, and I would suggest that despite these factors, Scotland's international football is 'bubbling' beneath the surface, ready to make a breakthrough.

In terms of relative populations, Scotland have done remarkably well in qualifying for the final stages in four successive World Cup competitions — Poland is the only other European country to have achieved such a feat without being the host country — but we still have to make the impact that other small nations such as Holland and Denmark have made at this level.

I feel, though, that we're capable of making such an impact, and it may not be too long before it's achieved. There's a tremendous pool of youthful talent waiting to be tapped by Scotland.

Celtic's Premier Division championship-winning side last season

Edinburgh referee Alistair Huett lectures Archie Knox in the Pittodrie dugout.

was a fairly young one and players such as Paul McStay, Derek Whyte, Joe Miller and Andy Walker all made significant contributions to the Parkhead club's success. Other home-based youngsters who come to mind in an international context include Derek Ferguson and Iain Durrant of Rangers and John Collins of Hibs.

There are lots of young Scots playing at the highest level in England, while those playing further afield on the Continent include former Don Eric Black, who, I think, has a very good chance of establishing himself in the full international side.

But we still have to master the knack of beating inferior opposition away from home. Maybe we should adopt the tactics of a club team playing away from home in a European tie and let the opposition attack, playing them on the break.

Against the lesser-known sides, the pressure is on Scotland because we're expected to beat them, so we go there and try to attack. But all these countries are well organised now, with German or Yugoslav coaches, and they can handle us on their own pitch. If

West Germany went to Malta, they wouldn't be employing all-out attack. They would stick to their usual studied football, knocking the ball about across the back and looking for the quick break.

If we can overcome this, I feel Scotland could make their mark in the European championship as well as the World Cup.

Back on the domestic front, an aspect of the Scottish game which surfaces from time to time is the question of crowd behaviour, or misbehaviour.

Fortunately, recent years have seen a big improvement, with the severe restrictions imposed on the availability of alcohol at the beginning of the decade playing a major role in that improvement, but it's still a worldwide problem for football authorities and we in Scotland can't afford to be complacent.

A more insidious threat, I feel, is the emergence of a new strain of the hooligan element, but as most of my thoughts about them are unprintable, I don't propose to comment further on louts who aren't interested in football as a sport, but merely as a stage for their mind-less mayhem.

The extent to which the behaviour of players on the field can pro-voke trouble on the terracings is the subject of much debate, with viewpoints being dictated by whether you're a player on the pitch or a supporter off it, but I received a salutary lesson in this matter a few years ago.

It was a match in which I scored for Aberdeen against Celtic at Pit-todrie, and as I returned to my position after scoring, I expressed my satisfaction by punching the air in a salute to Jim Leighton, who returned it in similar vein.

It was an unthinking gesture intended solely for the goalkeeper, but what I didn't realise was that it was interpreted by the Celtic sup-porters massed behind Jim's goal at the Beach End as a gesture of derision directed at them, and apparently it caused the police in that area of the ground a few anxious moments in containing the Celtic fans' reaction.

This was pointed out to me quite forcibly by an irate police super-intendent who sought me out in the dressing room after the game. He eventually accepted my explanation of my gesture, but drew my attention to its unfortunate consequences and warned me against any future repetition of such behaviour, no matter how innocent. I must say I took his point, filing it away as a valuable lesson.

While I'm very much in favour of any attempt to get footballers to

'Which way did it go?' Aerial study of Terry Butcher, one of the most successful of Rangers' English imports, and myself.

show a good example to the spectators by behaving well on the field, I have some reservations about the wisdom of making on-field behaviour a matter for the law courts, as happened last season.

The implications are far-reaching, and some of the possibilities opened up scarcely bear thinking about. There could be court cases arising from spectators reporting off-the-ball incidents to the police, and eventually we could have trial by television.

It would be better, I think, to leave on-field discipline entirely in the hands of the football authorities, who, if necessary, could increase the severity of the sanctions already in their power in suspensions, etc., to act as additional deterrent.

This brings us, of course, to referees, a vexed subject with most footballers, but one on which I can't make much comment. While appreciating that standards of refereeing vary from one individual to another — just as standards vary greatly among football players — there is one general observation I would like to make.

I feel that some referees could show more understanding in dealing with dissent. I know it's one of the areas in which the SFA have made special efforts to improve the situation, and quite rightly too, but some referees produce a yellow card as soon as a player opens his mouth, without allowing him even the breathing space of a warning.

Dissent is essentially a heat-of-the-moment offence which the player invariably regrets almost immediately, and in many cases, I feel, a word of warning from the referee would produce the desired effect.

Referees are not the only pet hates of footballers. The media, and the Press in particular, also come into this category, although I would say that it's more a love-hate relationship in this case, depending on whether the player is being praised or criticised.

This is something which affects a younger player more acutely, either raising or lowering his morale, but you learn to accept either praise or criticism in the newspapers and rely more on your own opinion of how you're playing. No-one knows better than the player himself whether he's playing well or badly.

In my own career, there have been times when I felt I wasn't getting full credit for my performances, but there have also been other times when I've felt that the praise I was given wasn't justified.

It's a case of swings and roundabouts, and you always have to remember that newspaper reports are usually subjective and that it's

Sponsorship has become an increasingly important feature of the Scottish game. Willie Miller and I act as models for the Dons' new strips following the sponsorship deal with JVC. Dons' chairman Dick Donald (right) and vice-chairman Ian Donald flank JVC chairman Kurt Lowry.

only the writer's own opinion you're reading, whether you agree with it or not.

Footballers frequently disagree with football writers' assessments. I remember Willie Miller being rather upset when newsmen made a great fuss of him after his performance against England at Wembley in 1981. He felt that he had performed equally well in earlier internationals but had been ignored by the Press, and he couldn't understand why he had suddenly come to their attention.

But sudden recognition of Willie's outstanding ability wasn't confined to the Press.

Morton's John McNeill, who was a colleague of mine in the Under-21 squad was not a Willie Miller fan until a Scotland game in Belgium in November, 1979. John and I had been on the bench for the Under-21s in Beveren the night before and we sat together watching the full Scotland team playing in Brussels.

Scotland were beaten 2-0 that night, but I thought Willie had a great game and this was backed up by John, who told me it had totally reversed his opinion of Willie as a player. But the Press weren't too complimentary about Willie's performance, and I remember, when he was complaining about this at breakfast the following morning, Bobby Clark telling him that he would have to develop a thick skin against adverse reports.

Newspaper speculation, too, is something you learn to take with a pinch of salt. Stories about such and such a club being interested in such and such a player obviously can have an unsettling effect on the player involved, but, on the other hand, I suppose it could give him a wee boost.

It never ceases to baffle me, though, how some of these speculative stories get started. The writers must either have a very good source of inside information or a very fertile imagination!

One thing about media coverage of football which does irritate me is the practice of some of television's soccer pundits from south of the Border — some of them exiled Scots — panning a Scotland performance almost as if they were enjoying our misfortunes. There was an extreme example of this in the live television coverage of our World Cup qualifying match in Australia. And in last April's friendly against Spain in Madrid, before a ball had been kicked, the commentator was predicting that the Scottish defence would give away a penalty in trying to keep control of Butragueno. In the event, I think we kept the tricky little Spanish striker reasonably quiet without having to resort to illegal tackles.

Mention of Spain and Butragueno reminds me of an earlier meeting with the Spaniards in Seville in February, 1985, during the qualifying stages of the 1986 World Cup.

Before leaving Scotland for that game I read an article on biorhythms, which are supposed to influence how a person performs in a particular activity at different times of the year. According to this review, my biorhythms were due to be at a low ebb at the time of the Seville game, which meant that I wouldn't have a good game.

Reading this rather nettled me and I was given extra motivation, if only to prove the theory was wrong. In the event, although we lost 1-0, I had what I would consider one of my best-ever games in a Scotland jersey, Butragueno and all. And just to confirm this, I was told later that Terry Venables, commenting on the game on TV, made me his 'man of the match'.

A clash typical of the Scottish game. I contest a high ball with Sandy Clark (Hearts).

It added to my satisfaction that some of the players who should have been in outstanding form according to the biorhythm theory didn't shine on that occasion.

To return to the media, though, I get on well with media people: they've got a job to do and they can play an important part in promoting football.

I've always been an avid reader of the sporting Press and at one time I was considering sports journalism as a career before professional football emerged as a possibility. Who knows, I might yet find a niche writing about football matches when I've finished playing in them!

One very important aspect of professional football in Scotland which I should mention is the role of the Professional Footballers' Association — the Players' Union, as it's sometimes called.

At one time, the Scottish PFA were well behind our English counterparts in both activity and organisation, but there has been an upsurge of interest in the Association among Scottish players in the last couple of years and I think we're begining to catch up on the English PFA in many respects.

Such a body is invaluable in helping players with financial and contractual problems and acting on their behalf in disputes, but probably its most important role is as a spokesman for the players, giving them a voice which might be listened to in football's corridors of power.

What has made a big difference, I think, has been having a former footballer as full-time secretary in Tony Higgins. Tony not only has had personal experience of the problems which can affect a professional footballer, but he's also highly articulate in speaking for us.

The future of Scottish football, of course, depends on a constant flow of young talent coming through to the league clubs. How long even the leading Scottish clubs can hold on to these players once they develop is another matter.

The one-time stream of players from Scotland to England and even further afield has, thankfully, slowed down in recent years, and, to a certain extent, has even been reversed, but it's inevitable that a proportion of the talent we produce will eventually be lost to the attractions offered by English or Continental clubs.

To succeed the stars who move on, clubs can sometimes buy ready-made replacements from a lower division, but a more reliable way is for clubs to 'grow their own' through an effective youth policy.

The problem then is how to ensure that you gather in enough of the right material at an early age to allow for natural wastage and still have left the players who have a real future in top-class football.

This is another reason why it's essential for a club like Aberdeen to be winning honours consistently. It gives their youth scouts an extra weapon when they're trying to sign the most promising young-sters in the face of competition from the Old Firm. The more suc-cessful a club is, the easier it is to 'sell' it to a prospective signing.

13

Unlucky For Some

I was going to discuss some of Scotland's football personalities in this chapter until I realised that it was Chapter 13. Some footballers are very superstitious, so I decided to follow the example of those managers who omit No. 13 on their team lists, and move on to Chapter 14.

14

Personality Parade

What makes a person a personality? The answers to that question are many, and you would probably get a different one from each person (or personality) you asked.

Pure footballing ability, of course, counts for a lot, but in my view a strong sense of humour is an important quality which contributes to the creation of a personality. Certainly, nearly all the footballers I've come across whom I would regard as being in that category have possessed a keen sense of humour.

Alan Rough, for instance, was always great fun to be with in international squads. You never got a chance to be bored when the big keeper was around.

I remember when we were in Australia for the World Cup qualifying match, we were invited to an official reception. We couldn't understand why Roughie was being so pally with one of our hosts and kept slapping him on the back. It was only when Alan's 'friend' — he was probably the local mayor or some such bigwig — walked away that we twigged. The shoulders of his jacket were liberally adorned with SFA stickers which Alan had attached under guise of his old pals act.

On another occasion, Roughie recruited some of his squadmates for one of his practical jokes. It consisted of him telling one of the Australians a 'funny' story which had a completely unfunny punchline, but we had to laugh heartily when he came out with it.

The first time Roughie told the story, the victim looked puzzled while we gave a passable impression of splitting our sides. 'Did ye no' get it?' asked Alan and proceeded to repeat the story with the same nonsensical punchline. Finally at the third telling, the Australian joined us in the laughter, although he obviously thought we were candidates for a lunatic asylum.

On our way home from Australia, we had a stopover at Dubai, and while doing some shopping there, Roughie borrowed £10 from me to buy a watch he fancied. Some time later when he came to Pittodrie with Hibs, I reminded him of the debt. 'Och, that watch disnae work now', was his reply, and I'm still waiting for my tenner.

The Australian trip was also the stage for a Roy Aitken-Alex McLeish con (or coin) trick. To while away a lengthy airport wait in Singapore, we armed ourselves with a pocketful of small change and one of us would toss one of the coins to land behind an unsuspecting passer-by who would immediately assume he had dropped the coin and would pick it up.

We did this several times to a Hong Kong businessman in the duty free shop, and although he was burdened with a suitcase, a shoulder bag and a carrier bag, he dutifully obliged each time by retrieving the coin, until eventually he began to check his pockets to see if they had a hole in them.

When he was joined by his young daughter, we overheard the businessman explaining the mystery of the dropping coins to her. 'The strange thing is that all the coins I pick up are Australian and I didn't have any of them in my pocket,' he said, while Roy and I tried to suppress our laughter as we innocently studied the duty free perfumes counter.

Roy and I used a variation of this joke on the way to Santa Fe before the 1986 World Cup finals. This time we had a dollar bill attached to a thin twine with a quick-winding mechanism at our end. The idea was to drop the note, stand some distance away, and then when someone bent to pick it up, press the release button and the note would flick back to you.

It was interesting to watch the different reactions to seeing a dollar note lying on the floor. Some would walk past it and then return to pick it up, others would stand over it and look round guiltily before casually bending down, and some, the wise guys, would recognise it right away as a trick.

Most of the victims joined in the laughter when they realised what was happening, but in Fort Worth Airport, a Texan, complete with big Stetson hat, was not amused.

After stopping his wife from trying to pick up the note, he looked round and identified Roy as the perpetrator of the trick. 'Sonny, you're a schmuck,' he said.

Practical jokes like those I've mentioned may seem a rather juvenile sense of humour, particularly when you read them on the printed page, and I suppose they are, but they're useful for relieving the tedium of long air trips when you frequently spend as much time hanging around airports as you do actually flying.

Those readers who know Roy Aitken only from his appearances on the football pitch, where he has a reputation as a hard man, might be surprised to learn of this light-hearted side of his personality.

Celtic's opponents' fans may not be too keen on Big Roy, and there's no love lost between him and myself when we're in opposition, but we're firm friends off the field. I think much of his 'hard man' image was built up in his younger days through tackles which were rash rather than malicious, and now that he's more mature, he isn't in trouble with referees so often. I know most Scottish footballers would rather have Roy Aitken in their side than in the opposition.

Professionalism is another quality which I would expect to find in a football personality, although some of the best examples of professionalism in the Scottish game are to be found in players who would never be thought of as personalities, nor would they claim to be.

I'm thinking of players who are rarely in the limelight, but produce sterling performances week after week. In the Dundee United team of a few years ago, for example, Iain Phillip and George Fleming were players in this category.

Of the Scottish players I've found myself in direct opposition to over the years, Celtic strikers figure prominently among those who have given Willie Miller and myself most trouble — and almost invariably they have operated most effectively in double harness with a particular partner.

There have been Charlie Nicholas and Frank McGarvey, Mo Johnston and Brian McClair and, most recently, Frank McAvennie and Andy Walker. Dave Dodds and Paul Sturrock were another dangerous pair when they were together with Dundee United.

In this respect, Rangers' Ally McCoist was something of an exception in that for much of last season he was a lone battler up front for the Ibrox side. But he always required careful watching.

Facing a striker, or a pair of strikers, who have high-scoring reputations is always an enjoyable challenge for a defender. Whether you come out on top or they do, there's always the next meeting to look forward to, when the situation might well be reversed.

15
My World XI

Thinking about the many fine footballers I've encountered in my career gave me the idea of choosing a World XI from the teams I've played against at either club or international level.

The more I reviewed the candidates for 'my team', with most positions having several contenders, the more difficult the job got to be.

In some cases, the choice of a particular player was eventually decided on tactical considerations such as how he would fit in with other players in the side, but in others, the player was a 'must' as far as I was concerned and went in without too much thought about the balance of the team — a sentimental rather than practical method of team selection, let's say.

Apart from restricting the choice to players I have actually played against, the only other ground rule I observed was that Scots were not eligible for inclusion.

Of all the top-class players I've shared a football pitch with, the one who impressed me most was, surprise, surprise, Michel Platini. It could be said that when we met, the French star left a deep impression on me in more senses than one. In fact, he left me speechless!

The occasion was Scotland's friendly against France in Marseilles in June, 1984, and although we weren't in direct opposition, I had an opportunity to appreciate the strength of his shot if nothing else.

At one point in the game he was presented with a close-range shooting opening and all I could do was to throw myself bodily in the path of the ball, receiving it full on the stomach from about three yards' range.

As I lay gasping for breath, I took some consolation in a perverse satisfaction from being winded by one of the world's best footballers of that time.

Actually, Platini was not particularly outstanding in that game, but I had long been an admirer of his play.

I remember watching France winning the 1984 European championships while I was on holiday in Portugal and found myself in the company of quite a number of other footballers from both Scotland and England. In fact, when we gathered in a bar one evening we worked out that we had enough to pick two full teams, complete with manager, coach and physio — and we even had a football writer from a national daily newspaper in the company.

But watching the championships on television made us all realise just how influential Platini was in that French team. So Platini would be the first to find a place in my World XI, and several of his team-mates in the French side that night would also be in contention, particularly Jean Tigana and Alain Giresse.

Giresse, so difficult for an opponent to pin down, was probably the best French player in the Marseilles game, and he scored the first of France's two goals against us, while Tigana's play was pure poetry. He seemed to have the uncanny knack of dispossessing an opponent without even tackling him.

But I mustn't start off my team selection with the midfield. Let's go back and start with the goalkeeper.

There are some outstanding keepers on the Continent, but I haven't been too impressed with any I've played against, and honestly I can't see past British players for this position. As Scots are excluded, I would be swithering between Englishmen Ray Clemence and Peter Shilton, with the former having a slight edge in my estimation, possibly because I've played against him more often than Shilton.

One of my full backs would certainly be Marcel Amoros, another member of that French team of the Marseilles friendly. The Monaco defender is an exciting player who likes to get forward. He could play on either flank, but as I've chosen Manni Kaltz (S V Hamburg) as the other full back, I'll have Amoros on the left.

In Kaltz, we would have another full back who is tremendous going forward and, like most West Germans, his crossing on the run is impressive. Any defects he had defensively tended to be forgotten because he was so good in attack.

For central defenders, some might think Franz Beckenbauer would be an obvious choice. I had the good fortune to play against the Kaiser before the time came to hang up his boots, and although the legs were beginning to go, his class was still apparent.

However, I've decided to bypass the West German superstar for my team because I didn't see as much of him at close quarters as I did some other central defenders. Instead, I'm suggesting a partnership between Spain's Antonio Maceda and Gothenburg's Glen

Hysen, which I think would be an interesting pairing.

I first came across Maceda during our World Cup qualifying campaign and was most impressed. I met him again when we played Spain in a friendly in Madrid last season. Apparently he had moved from Seville to Real Madrid but had been out of the game for about a year, and he was in the dressing room after training on his own when we visited Real's training ground.

Maceda came to the fore in the 1984 European championships when Spain got to the final before losing to France. For a very tall player — about 6ft 3in or 6ft 4in — he was very skilful on the ground and a contrast to the more physical play of his central defensive partner, Andoni Goicochea, who became known as the 'Butcher of Bilbao'.

I would like to see Maceda's silky play allied to the Swede Hysen, who is now playing in Italy. Hysen is more like the British-type centre half in that he's very aggressive in the air as well as a strong tackler.

Now we're back to the midfield, and after a great deal of head-scratching I've settled on Platini's partners. Fellow-Frenchman Giresse is one and the other is Brazil's Zico. That may be cheating a little bit as I played only twenty minutes against him when I came on as a substitute in Scotland's meeting with Brazil in the 1982 World Cup finals, but it would be worth stretching a point to have a player like Zico in my side.

Choosing the front men is equally difficult: there are so many who, for different reasons, would be contenders.

The Continental striker who gave me the hardest time over one game was Gothenburg's Torbjorn Nilsson, but then there's Porto's Fernando Gomes, who is usually in the running for the Golden Boot scoring award, while the Danish pair, Preben Elkjaer and Michael Laudrup, have reputations which speak for themselves.

When we played Denmark in Mexico, Laudrup was not too prominent, but he demonstrated his incredible pace on a couple of occasions. I remember once when I had moved forward and left myself exposed, he stuck the ball past me and the only way I could stop him breaking was with an Italian-style body check.

There was another instance in the second half when Maurice Malpas seemed to have plenty of time for a safe pass-back to Jim Leighton in goal when Laudrup, who had been ten to twenty yards away, suddenly descended on him and Maurice was saved from an uncomfortable situation only by having a free kick awarded when the Dane made contact with him.

To return to my selection, I eventually plumped for the combination of Nilsson and Ian Rush as the main strike force to see how Rush, one of the best finishers I've ever seen, would profit from the through passes of Platini. Nilsson, I feel, would be a good foil for the Welshman. The Swede is much more than just a target man. He's strong, skilful and quick.

That left only a decision whether to field an extra midfield man or a winger. Wingers are almost a dying breed these days, although there are some signs that they're coming back into favour again.

I toyed with the idea of having Spain's Emilio Butragueno playing off the front two to set up chances for them if Platini wasn't getting his passes through, but finally settled on another Spaniard in Rafael Gordillo to play as a deep-lying left-sided player who could get to the bye-line.

Thank goodness for the allowance of five substitutes, because naming that number gives me a chance to include some of the players I swithered over for places in the starting line-up.

Shilton would be my substitute goalkeper and there would also be places on the bech for Tigana, Butragueno and Gomes, with Bayern Munich's Paul Breitner as the defensive sub.

Just to remind you, here's the line-up I finally arrived at: Clemence; Kaltz, Hysen, Maceda, Amoros; Zico, Platini, Giresse, Gordillo; Nilsson, Rush.

Subs: Shilton, Breitner, Tigana, Butragueno, Gomes.

It's quite an internationl squad, isn't it! And there are almost as many great players again that I haven't even mentioned who could have been included, particularly in the striking department. Apart from the Danes Elkjaer and Laudrup, there are West Germans in Klaus Allofs and Karl Heinz Rumenigge, to say nothing of the Belgians.

Some readers might be asking, for instance, why I haven't included Nico Claesen, who scored a hat-trick for Belgium against Scotland in Brussels last year. But that was just a game which was ideally suited for him and, as I've already mentioned, I felt our tactics were all wrong. I don't rate Claesen as highly as the players I've selected.

Claesen didn't give us the same trouble in the return game at Hampden simply because our tactics were sounder, and, in fact, we beat Belgium 2-0.

Looking at my selection tactically, I think my midfield might be lacking a bit in balance, but, overall, it's a team I would like to see playing together.

I still have to think about who would provide worthy opposition for such a hypothetical team, but if a game could be arranged for them, there is only one person to have as referee — Willie Miller!

16

If I Can Help . . .

I'm told that in a large public office in Aberdeen, the staff run a sweep on which page of the *Press and Journal* my picture will appear on any particular day.

I don't know if the story is true, but it's an indication of how regularly my face, battle-scarred as it is, appears in that newspaper — and more often that not on the news rather than the sports pages.

On most of these occasions I'm pictured receiving a cheque from this or that firm on behalf of Linn Moor Residential School for handi-

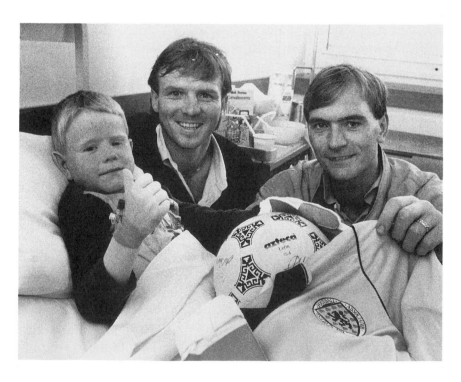

Jim Leighton and I visit a young Dons' fan in hospital.

With Mrs Jean Argo, head teacher at Linn Moor.

capped childen, with whom I've had a close association in recent years.

It's quite common for charity organisations to invite footballers to assist them in fund-raising schemes. It doesn't involve the player in much effort beyond making himself available from time to time to have his photograph taken when large donations are being handed over, and helping in other ways to publicise whatever project the charity is currently engaged in.

I suppose there are some players who regard such demands on their time as a chore, the price of prominence, if you like, but the vast majority are only too happy to lend their names (and faces) in support of a worthy cause, and, in fact, feel flattered to be asked.

It can also be very satisfying to feel that in some small way you've contributed to helping someone who is less fortunate than yourself.

The requests are varied, ranging from breaking bottles of coins and opening coffee mornings and summer fêtes to playing in pro-amateur golf events.

The Aberdeen club's association with Linn Moor goes back some time, and when the school embarked more than two years ago on an ambitious campaign to raise something like £400,000 to improve their facilities, I was invited to 'front' the venture. Permission was readily given by Alex Ferguson, who was manager at the time, provided, of course, that it didn't interfere with my football commitments.

An initial target of £70,000 was set for the first stage of the campaign to test the public response and, happily, that figure was achieved in a remarkably short time, so it was decided to continue the project.

Public houses, commercial films, organisations, and private individuals have all contributed (and are continuing to contribute) magnificently, while the local newspapers, the *Press and Journal* and the *Evening Express,* have also played their part by giving the campaign generous publicity.

Some of the money-raising ideas have been imaginative to say the least, such as a golf marathon in which youngsters set out at the crack of dawn in an attempt to play six rounds of golf before darkness fell. Other people have cycled the length of the country.

It all goes to prove that the reputation Aberdeen people have for being mean is indeed only a joke.

For me, the most rewarding aspect of the exercise has been a closer acquaintance with the children and staff at Linn Moor, and with a better understanding of the problems they face has come a deeper admiration for the way they cope with these problems.

I used to visit the school before my involvement with the present fund-raising campaign, but, obviously, my visits are more frequent now and I've come to know the children quite well and to be recognised by them. They come from all parts of Scotland and many of them are Rangers and Celtic supporters, but I think I've managed to make some converts so that most of them have at least a soft spot for the Dons!

One evening when I was driving home about 9.30, I saw a solitary figure walking along North Deeside Road. The youngster seemed familiar, but it was only after I'd turned off the main road into my own street that I realised it had been Barry, one of the Linn Moor teenagers with whom I had been pictured for one of the publicity posters.

I turned the car round and caught up with Barry and discovered that he had been in town playing snooker and had missed the bus

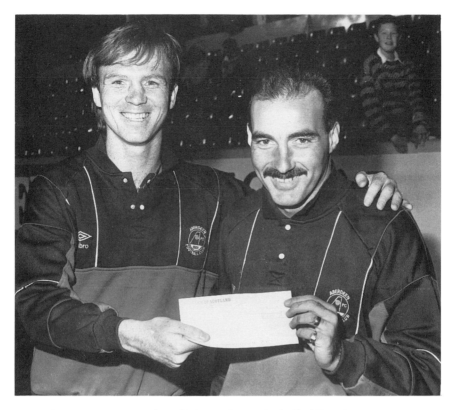

I receive a cheque from Willie Miller on behalf of Pittodrie players.

home. This 16-year-old was cheerfully setting out to walk the seven or eight miles to the school in Culter. But he was glad to accept my offer of a lift.

That's the kind of independent resourcefulness many of these handicaped youngsters show.

But I remember one occasion when one of the Linn Moor youngsters gave me a real fright. On one of my visits to the school this young lad asked me to give him a run in my car. Mrs Argo, the head teacher, warned me that this particular youngster was apt to touch anything and everything that came within his reach.

'I don't think there's anything he can do much damage to', said I unthinkingly, but the youngster didn't take long to prove me wrong. We were bowling along about 20 m.p.h. in a circuit of the school block when his hand shot out and pulled the gear lever (it was an automatic car I was running at the time) from forward into reverse.

Trying out the school mini-bus along with one of the pupils.

I don't know which of us got the bigger shock!

My association with Linn Moor has received a lot of publicity because it's a campaign, but there's a lot of charitable work done by footballers which the general public never hear about, such as visiting children in hospital and spending some time with them. It would be difficult to decide who enjoys these occasions most, the visited or the visitor.

I know that the Linn Moor appeal being a children's charity makes it particularly attractive to me, having children of my own, but I think that most footballers feel the same, whether they're fathers or not.

I remember when we were in Mexico City for the 1986 World Cup finals, Alan Rough and I just about emptied our pockets of dollars giving them to the beggar women who sat on the pavement with their children either lying in their arms or playing in the dust beside them.

We knew very well that these women were exploiting both their own children and our sympathy, and we used to joke that after a profitable day's begging they probably went home in a huge car to a palatial house, but we couldn't resist the appeals of those who had children with them, as, indeed, most of them did, as an essential 'prop.'

Who said that footballers aren't soft-hearted?

17

Family and Future

Children mean a great deal to me, and none more so than my own two boys, seven-year-old Jon and Jamie, who is three.

When Jon was born, my wife Jill and I, novices in the art of bringing up children, were probably over-protective and we wrapped him in cotton wool, figuratively speaking. In the four years before Jamie came along, however, we learned a lot and we were more relaxed with him. As a result, Jamie is a wee wild man compared to how angelic his older brother was. That may have been because

'That's my dad,' says Jon (extreme right) as he and his schoolmates present me with a cheque for Linn Moor after a fund-raising effort.

Do you like my style in headgear!

when Jon was small, we seemed to be short of boys in the neigh-
bourhood and most of his friends were girls.

Generally, the two boys get on well together, but now that Jon is
at school and has his own pals, Jamie cramps his style a bit.
Although there is a gap in their ages, it's almost as if we had twins
when it comes to buying them toys, for anything that Jon gets,
Jamie wants the same.

As far as football is concerned, Jamie has always been mad keen
on a ball, but it's only in the last couple of years since Jill started taking him with her to matches that Jon has begun to take an interest in
football. Again that may be due to having mainly girls as his early
playmates.

But he has a good eye for a ball and he's making up for lost time
and wants the full gear — trainers, strips, and now, football boots.

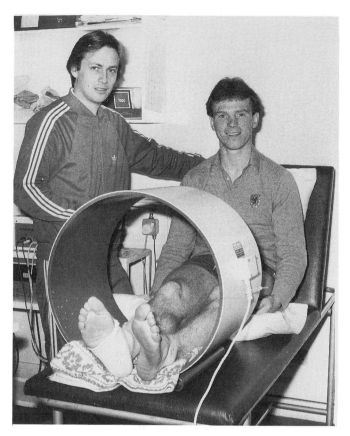

Roland Arnott the club physio is putting me through the hoop.

I'm determined not to push the boys into any particular sport the way my father pushed me in my early football career, to the extent that we sometimes fell out.

Mind you, that early pressure did me no harm, but I would prefer to let the boys sample a variety of sports and make a choice for themselves.

All the same, I sometimes find myself coaching Jon when we're kicking a ball about, so I suppose I'm very like my dad in many ways. I know if I went to watch Jon play in a match, I would shout at him exactly as my dad did with me — 'Bawling Alex' my mates used to call him.

As I mentioned before, I have a sister, Angela, who works in an aunt's printing firm, and a brother, Ian, who's an apprentice painter

I am welcomed back from the 1986 World Cup finals by wife Jill and baby Jamie.

and decorator. Ian has become a devoted Dons' fan, and there's no living with him when we lose a game.

Ian is not the only one in the family to take a keen interest in the activities of Aberdeen FC in general and myself in particular. I would say, in fact, that Jill and the other female members of the family — my sister, my mother, and two, yes, two, grannies — take it much harder than I do myself if I'm criticised in the Press.

One of my grannies, my mother's mother, is particularly proud of me and likes to show me off to anyone who'll listen. Once when I was with her, I was asked for my autograph, whereupon she introduced herself as 'Alex's granny' to the autograph hunter, who made her his friend for life by telling her she didn't look old enough.

After that, she incorporated the compliment into her own remarks by saying 'I'm Alex McLeish's granny, although I don't look it.' She'a quite a character!

Jill and Jon see me off on way to Portugal.

Although not strictly a member of my family, there's someone I should mention in this chapter, such was the closeness of his friendship with the McLeish family.

Kenny Haldane was my father's best pal and, like him, a devoted Rangers supporter. My dad didn't drive and Kenny used to take us about in his car. When I was a boy we often went to Rouken Glen on a Sunday afternoon where Kenny and my dad played football with me — toughening me up as Kenny used to say later.

When dad started following Aberdeen to watch me play, Kenny was again the driver and he soon became as keen a Dons' supporter as his passenger.

Kenny took my father's death particularly hard and he became almost like a second father to us, taking Ian to games and he and his wife Margaret frequently spending weekends with Jill and me in Aberdeen.

Another of my father's constant companions at Dons' games was Tam Healy, a boyhood pal of mine, and when I got together with my dad, Kenny and Tam, their patter was simply hilarious.

Jill and I inspect the
Scottish Cup.

Sadly, though, Kenny also died quite young a few years ago, and although Tam is still an Aberdeen supporter, I don't see quite so much of him nowadays.

An aspect of my job which sometimes upsets the female side of the family is my susceptibility to injury. As a central defender, of course, many of these injuries are to the head and face, particularly round the eyes, and I've lost count of the number of facial stitches I've had in the course of my career.

It has become something of a family joke, and not only in the family. If, for example, I come across Billy McNeill when I have a plaster on my face, he's bound to wind me up with something like: 'Stitches again? You must be losing your touch in the air', to which my stock reply is: 'No, it's these centre forwards. They canna jump!'

Over the years, Jill has become almost hardened to the sight of

Our first-born Jon.

A little older — and wiser — with Jamie.

Head-to-head
with brother Ian.

me returning home with stitches in an eyebrow, and the only thing
that worries her now is a leg or an internal injury, which, she knows,
can be a longer-term affair.

Face cuts, most of them on top of an old cut, do nothing to
improve my looks, which were nothing to boast about in the first
place, although Jill insists they add 'character' to my face. As the
sting in the tail, she then adds: 'And the character is Quasimodo'.

Then there's my crooked nose. The only occasion I can remember sustaining an actual nose break was long ago when I clashed
with Colin McAdam and his famous flying elbows. I should have had
it set then, but I think we were going abroad a couple of days later
and I did nothing about it — but most of the damage, I suppose, has
been caused by a succession of minor knocks.

I'm at the stage now when I wouldn't mind too much having my

A family portrait with wife Jill and sons Jon (aged 7) and Jamie (aged 3).

nose broken so that I can get it re-set properly. In fact, in on-field exchanges with opposing strikers I often take them aback by inviting them to break my nose — providing they're careful to break it from the right side to knock the bone straight again. Any centre forwards reading this can accept it as an open invitation.

My battered countenance once led to someone mistaking my profession. I happened to be visiting an Aberdeen hotel on the morning after a Scotland-Ireland amateur boxing international in the city.

Two of the Irish boxing officials who were staying at the hotel kept looking at me as I sat in the lounge waiting for a friend. 'Ah, they know their football', I thought. 'They've recognised me.' My fond illusions of fame, however, were shattered when eventually one of them came over and in the broadest brogue hailed me with: 'Weren't you boxing against us last night?'

The most amusing reaction to my injuries comes from my younger son, Jamie, whose comment 'You get sore eye' may be a statement of the obvious but sounds funny when developed into a repetitive chant.

There was one time when we thought Jamie showed a prophetic gift. As I was saying good-bye to him when Jill dropped me off at Pittodrie for a match, he said 'Daddy get sore eye', and sure enough, I came home from that game with more stitches. In his young mind, seeing his dad leave for a match was evidently linked in some way with sore eyes.

In these days when it seems that public houses must have a distinctive name, I'll have no difficulty naming mine if I ever go into the licensed trade. It will be called 'Stitches.'

Mention of the possibility of owning a pub brings me on to the question of my future.

'What am I going to do?' was a question I often asked myself as I neared the end of my schooldays, never dreaming that the answer would come in the shape of a career in professional football.

I'm not quite yet at the stage of asking myself the same question again, but the day is coming when I will have to give serious consideration to what happens after football. The answer could well be: 'more football — but in a different capacity'. At the moment, though, I'm keeping my options open.

I want to make provision outside football with business interests of some kind, but I'm also currently taking coaching qualifications at Largs which would be useful if I continue in the game, although obviously they don't guarantee you a job.

Having gone to Largs for the past two years, I can appreciate now the type of drills that Alex Ferguson and Archie Knox used to give us and I can see that they were of especial benefit to the forward players such as Eric Black, Steve Archibald, Mark McGhee and John Hewitt and wing men like Peter Weir and Gordon Strachan.

Fergie and Archie used to have us practising crossing and finishing until we could have done it in our sleep, but it certainly paid dividends. They worked a lot with the forwards and made them relate to each other instead of playing as individuals, and this, I believe, was their forte.

I stress, though, that we were young players at that time and this is clearly the best stage to receive coaching.

The Largs courses are very worthwhile. The methods are laid

down very simply, and once you get the confidence in speaking to and organising your group of players, then you're halfway to qualifying.

The courses bring together the pros and the amateurs with the common ambition of being good coaches. I can assure the amateurs that it's just as nerve-racking for the pros as for you.

Members of the courses are split into groups and each individual gets a chance to lead his group, in other words to be the coach.

In my first year there, Gordon Strachan, Eamonn Bannon and I were in the same group. Wee Gordon was late for the pre-session warm-up, and the bloke who was coach — having been wound up by someone, I wonder who! — screamed at him: 'Strachan, get your ..... up here!'

When Gordon jogged up to join us, the coach then shouted: 'Get doon and gie us ten (press-ups).' The coach, whoever he is, must be obeyed, so Gordon had to suffer his punishment dutifully, if not exactly cheerfully.

On another occasion when one of the amateurs was coach to a group which included Roy Aitken, he caused a few laughs when, in the course of his team talk, his instruction to the Celtic skipper was: 'Roy, just boot it up the park early. You canna use the ba'.'

To return to thoughts about my future, I think I'm reasonably knowledgeable about football and, after serving under a few different managers, I've learned a lot that I could put to good use in football management.

But that's all in the future. I'll be 31 by the time my current contract with Aberdeen expires in two years' time, but I feel I can go on for a few years yet. I would like to keep playing for as long as possible.

After all, you're a long time no' playin'!

My Playing Record

Aug 2, 1977 — First-team debut as sub for Willie Garner in pre-season friendly against Fraserburgh at Bellslea Park. Aberdeen lost 0-3.

Jan 2, 1978 — Competitive debut in New Year league game v Dundee Utd at Pittodrie. Aberdeen won 1-0.

Sept 29, 1979 — 50th first-team appearance in league match v Dundee at Dens Park. Aberdeen won 4-0.

Aug 16, 1980 — 100th appearance in league match against Dundee Utd at Pittodrie. 1-1 draw.

May 22, 1982 — 200th appearance in Scottish Cup final against Rangers at Hampden Park. Scored first of Aberdeen's goals in 4-1 victory after extra time.

April 6, 1983 — 250th appearance in European Cup-Winners' Cup semi-final (first leg) against Waterschei (Belgium) at Pittodrie. Aberdeen won 5-1.

Dec 17, 1983 — 300th appearance in league game against Hibs at Pittodrie. Aberdeen won 2-1.

Oct 12, 1985 — 400th appearance in league game against Hibs at Easter Road. 1-1 draw.

Sept 15, 1987 — 500th appearance in UEFA Cup first round (first leg) against Bohemians in Dublin. 0-0 draw.

FIRST TEAM GOALS — 32
League — 23
League Cup — 1
Scottish Cup — 2
European ties — 1
Friendlies — 5

EUROPEAN APPEARANCES — 45

1978-79 — Cup Winners' Cup
1st Rd (2nd leg) — Marek Dimitrov (h) 3-0
2nd Rd (1st leg) — Fortuna Düsseldorf (a) 0-3
       (2nd leg) — Fortuna Düsseldorf (h) 2-0

1979-80 — UEFA Cup
   1st Rd (2nd leg) — Eintracht Frankfurt (a) 0-1

1980-81 — European Cup
   1st Rd (1st leg) — Austria Memphis (h) 1-0
   2nd Rd (1st leg) — Liverpool (h) 0-1
          (2nd leg) — Liverpool (a) 0-4

1981-82 — UEFA Cup
   1st Rd (1st leg) — Ipswich (holders) (a) 1-1
          (2nd leg) — Ipswich   (h) 3-1
   2nd Rd (2nd leg) — Arges Pitesti (a) 2-2
   3rd Rd (2nd leg) — SV Hamburg (a) 1-3

1982-83 — Cup Winners' Cup
   Prelim Rd (1st leg) — FC Sion (h) 7-0
            (2nd leg) — FC Sion (a) 4-1 (sub for Bell)
   1st Rd (2nd leg) — Dinamo Tirana (a) 0-0
   2nd Rd (1st leg) — Lech Poznan (h) 2-0
          (2nd leg) — Lech Poznan (a) 1-0
   Quarter-final (1st leg) — Bayern Munich (a) 0-0
                (2nd leg) — Bayern Munich (h) 3-2 (scored goal)
   Semi-final (1st leg) — Waterschei (h) 5-1 (250th app)
             (2nd leg) — Waterschei (a) 0-1
   Final — Real Madrid in Gothenburg 2-1 (aet)

1983-84 — Cup Winners' Cup
   1st Rd (1st leg) — Akranes (a) 2-1
          (2nd leg) — Akranes (h) 1-1
   2nd Rd (1st leg) — SK Beveren (a) 0-0
          (2nd leg) — SK Beveren (h) 4-1
   Quarter-final (1st leg) — Ujpest Dozsa (a) 0-2
                (2nd leg) — Ujpest Dozsa (h) 3-0 (booked)
   Semi-final (1st leg) — Porto (a) 0-1
             (2nd leg) — Porto (h) 0-1

      Super Cup
   1st leg — SV Hamburg (a) 0-0
   2nd leg — SV Hamburg (h) 2-0

1984-85 — European Cup
1st Rd (1st leg) — Dinamo Berlin (h) 2-1
        (2nd leg) — Dinamo Berlin (a) 1-2 (lost 4-5 on pen)

1985-86 — European Cup
1st Rd (1st leg) — Akranes (a) 3-1
        (2nd leg) — Akranes (h) 4-1
2nd Rd (1st leg) — Servette (a) 0-0
        (2nd leg) — Servette (h) 1-0
Quarter-final (1st leg) — IFK Gothenburg (h) 2-2
              (2nd leg) — IFK Gothenburg (a) 0-0 (lost on away goals rule)

1986-87 — Cup Winners' Cup
1st Rd (1st leg) — FC Sion (h) 2-1
        (2nd leg) — FC Sion (a) 0-3

1987-88 — UEFA Cup
1st Rd (1st leg) — Bohemians (a) 0-0 (500th app)
        (2nd leg) — Bohemians (h) 1-0
2nd Rd (1st leg) — Feyenoord (h) 2-1
        (2nd leg) — Feyenoord (a) 0-1 (lost on away goals rule)

INTERNATIONAL APPEARANCES

55 Full caps
6 Under-21 caps
1 B cap

1977-78 — Under-21 v Wales (Feb 8)

1978-79 — Under-21 v United States (Sep 17)

1979-80 — Under-21 v Belgium (Dec 18), Under-21 v England (Feb 12), Under-21 v England (Mar 4), Portugal (Mar 26) (first full cap), N. Ireland (May 16), Wales (May 21), England (May 24), Poland (May 28), Hungary (May 31).

1980-81 — Sweden (Sep 10), Israel (Feb 25), N. Ireland (Mar 25), Israel (Apr 28), N. Ireland (May 19), England (May 23).

1981-82 — Sweden (Sep 9), Spain (Feb 24), N. Ireland (Apr 28), Brazil (June 18) (sub 68 min).

1982-83 — Belgium (Dec 15), Switzerland (Mar 30) (sub 45 min), Wales (May 28), England (June 1), Canada (June 12), Canada (June 16), Canada (June 19).

1983-84 — Uruguay (Sept 21), Belgium (Oct 12), E. Germany (Nov 16), N. Ireland (Dec 13), Wales (Feb 28), England (May 26), France (June 1).

1984-85 — Yugoslavia (Sep 12), Iceland (Oct 17), Spain (Nov 14), Spain (Feb 27), Wales (Mar 27), England (May 25), Iceland (May 28).

1985-86 — Wales (Sep 10), E. Germany (Oct 16), Australia (Nov 20) (40th full cap), Australia (Dec 4), England (Apr 23), Holland (Apr 29), Denmark (June 4).

1986-87 — Under-21 (over-age and capt) v Eire (Feb 17), Belgium (Apr 1), France B (capt) (Apr 28), England (May 23), Brazil (May 26).

1987-88 — Belgium (Oct 14), Bulgaria (Nov 11), Luxembourg (Dec 2) (capt to mark 50th full cap), Saudi Arabia (Feb 17) (sub 45 min), Malta (Mar 22), Spain (Apr 27), Colombia (May 17), England (May 21).

FIRST-TEAM APPEARANCES

Season	L	LC	SC	AC	EC	CWC	UEFA	ESC	DC	F	Totals
1977-78	1									3(1)	4(1)
1978-79	19(1)	4(1)	3(2)			3					29(4)
1979-80	35	11	4				1		1(1)	5	57(1)
1980-81	32	5	2	1	3				3	6	52
1981-82	32	8	6				4			8	58
1982-83	34(1)	7	5			10(1)				4	60(2)
1983-84	32	10	7			8		2		11(1)	70(1)
1984-85	30	1	6(1)		2					7	46(1)
1985-86	34	6	6		6					8	60
1986-87	40	3	3			2				7	55
1987-88	35	2	5				4			5	51
Totals	324(2)	57(1)	47(3)	1	11	23(1)	9	2	4(1)	64(2)	542 (10)

L = League
LC = League Cup
SC = Scottish Cup
AC = Aberdeenshire Cup
EC = European Cup
CWC = Cup-Winners Cup
ESC = European Super Cup
DC = Drybrough Cup
F = Friendlies

* Figures include substitute appearances. Sub appearances indicated in brackets.

Index